RHETORIC FOR LEGAL WRITERS

THE THEORY AND PRACTICE OF ANALYSIS AND PERSUASION

Second Edition

■ ■ ■

Kristen Konrad Tiscione

Professor, Legal Research and Writing
Georgetown University Law Center
Washington, D.C.

AMERICAN CASEBOOK SERIES®

WEST
ACADEMIC
PUBLISHING

American Casebook Series is a trademark registered in the U.S. Patent and Trademark Office.

© 2009 Thomson Reuters
© 2016 LEG, Inc. d/b/a West Academic
     444 Cedar Street, Suite 700
     St. Paul, MN 55101
     1-877-888-1330

West, West Academic Publishing, and West Academic are trademarks of West Publishing Corporation, used under license.

Printed in the United States of America

ISBN: 978-1-63460-266-2

To Nick, who is everything, and
Vicki, for her love and support.

PREFACE

When I learned to ride a bike, I did not just hop on and start pedaling. First, my father explained to me what to do and why: "You'll need to hold the wheel straight," "Pedal fast enough to keep the bike going," and "Don't slam on the brakes, or you'll go flying." When I got on the bike, he held it steady. As I started to pedal, he held on until I was going fast enough to keep the bike up (apparently he subscribed to the "no training wheels" philosophy). As I pedaled, I began to understand what he meant by needing to pedal fast enough. If I didn't, I started to lose balance. Once I realized he had let go, I got scared and slammed on the brakes. Then I understood what he meant by "you'll go flying."

Theory informs practice, which informs theory. The two are inseparable. Knowing the theory of bike riding helped me learn to ride a bike. Similarly, knowing the theory of legal analysis and persuasion will help you learn to be a good legal writer and lawyer. This book introduces you to the what, the why, and the how of legal writing. The source of the theory is classical and contemporary rhetoric. Rhetoric is the study of human communication and persuasion. It dates back to ancient Greece and was taught all over the world for thousands of years. The scope of its subject matter was dramatically reduced during the Renaissance, and its influence on education in the Western world began to wane. It survived during the eighteenth century as the study of speaking and writing style, but by the end of the nineteenth century, it had disappeared.

When I first wrote this book (which took several years), I was relatively new to rhetoric. As a young professor, I stumbled across it during the course of my research on persuasive legal writing. I had majored in English in college, graduated from law school, and practiced law for many years, but I had never even heard of it. I realize now how painfully obvious it was that I was new to the discipline. Rhetoric explained so much about what I had struggled to learn that I wanted to share my newfound knowledge with students. So I crammed as much as I could into the book, and the result was a bit overwhelming.

This second edition reads like an entirely different book. I have taken out much of the extraneous material and tried to retain just enough history for context and only the core concepts. I tried to slow down the pace of the book and explain better the core concepts. I have added a chapter on learning to be a law student and sections on conducting legal research, writing complaints, client letters, and bench memos, reporting on the results of research, and meeting with clients. My hope is to have achieved a better balance between theory and practice in a more accessible text.

I do not profess to be an expert in philosophy or rhetoric, nor do readers of this book need to be. That's the whole point of the book: to explain the theory that informs the practice of law to hasten and improve your learning. I hope I have done a better job this time around. As you face the challenges of learning to think, write, and speak like a lawyer, recognize that you may "go flying" a few times. We've all been there. Just climb back on that bike and start pedaling. It's quite a wonderful ride.

KRISTEN K. TISCIONE
Professor, Legal Research and Writing
Georgetown University Law Center

December 2015

ACKNOWLEDGMENTS

One sabbatical, two research leaves, and several summer writing grants have helped make this book possible. I am grateful to **Deans Alexander Aleinikoff and William Treanor** for Georgetown University Law Center's unflagging financial support of my scholarship. I am also grateful to the following faculty and colleagues, whose advice and expertise proved invaluable for both editions:

Noelle Adgerson, Executive Assistant, Legal Research and Writing, Georgetown. University Law Center

Wayne Davis, Philosophy Department Chair and Professor, Georgetown University

Jennifer Locke Davitt, Head of Faculty Services, Georgetown Law Library, Georgetown University Law Center

Frances C. DeLaurentis, Professor, Legal Research and Writing, Georgetown University Law Center

Vicki Girard, Professor, Legal Research and Writing, Georgetown University Law Center

Dee Konrad, Professor of English, Barat College

Betsy Kuhn, Faculty Editor, Georgetown University Law Center

Ellie Margolis, Professor of Law, Temple University Beasley School of Law

Heather McCabe, Associate Professor, Legal Research and Writing, Georgetown University Law Center and partner, McCabe Russell, P.A.

Jarrod Reich, Associate Professor, Legal Research and Writing, Georgetown University Law Center

Ruth Anne Robbins, Clinical Professor, Rutgers Law

Jill A. Smith, Instructional Technology Librarian, Georgetown University Law Center

Louis Michael Seidman, Carmack Waterhouse Professor of Constitutional Law, Georgetown University Law Center

Anna Selden, Associate Director of Publications, Georgetown University Law Center

Morgan Stoddard, Research Services Librarian and Adjunct Professor of Law, Georgetown University Law Center

Robin West, Frederick J. Haas Professor of Law and Philosophy, Georgetown University Law Center

I thank my tireless research assistants, *Amanda Rome, Gabriel Lerner* (in memoriam), *Margaret Engoren, Jonathan Ammons, Rex Winter,* and now *Molly Clarke* (second edition), whose hard work and enthusiasm over the years has helped sustain me. Finally, I thank my husband for his stalwart belief in me and my passion for rhetoric.

If ancient Greece and Rome are dust,
we are but wind to keep them aloft.

SUMMARY OF CONTENTS

PREFACE V

ACKNOWLEDGMENTS VII

Chapter 1. Introduction to Law School.. 1
1. Welcome to the Legal Profession 1
2. What Are Legal Research and Legal Writing? 2
3. How Does Legal Research and Writing Differ from Other First-Year
    Courses? 6
4. How Do You Read for Class? 7
5. What Do Your Professors Expect of You? 13

Chapter 2. Law and Rhetoric.. 15
1. What Is Rhetoric? 15
2. A Brief History of Rhetoric 17
3. Why Don't Law Schools Teach Rhetoric? 36
4. Law as Rhetoric 39
5. Do Objective Rules of Law Exist Out There Somewhere? 41

Chapter 3. The Rhetorical Process.. 47
1. Aristotle's Canons of Rhetoric 47
2. What Is Writing, or How Were You Taught to Write?.............. 49
3. Take Time to Assess Your Research and Writing Persona 53

Chapter 4. Discovering Arguments.. 57
1. Sources of Law 57
2. Statutory Interpretation 58
3. Hierarchy of Authority 61
4. Print and Online Resources 65
5. The Research Process 69
6. Organize and Analyze as You Go 75

Chapter 5. Appeals to Reason.. 79
1. The Analytical Paradigm 79
2. Induction (Rule Synthesis) 80
3. Deduction (Legal Syllogisms) 87
4. Fallacies in Deductive Reasoning 97
5. A Modern Take on the Legal Syllogism 101
6. Analogical Reasoning 103
7. Fallacies in Analogical Reasoning.. 106
8. Narrative Reasoning 109
9. Policy-Based Reasoning 111

Chapter 6. Legal Advice and Predictive Writing.................................. 115
1. What Is Predictive Writing? 115
2. Appeals to *Pathos* in Predictive Writing................................. 116
3. Appeals to *Ethos* in Predictive Writing................................... 117

Chapter 7. Arrangement in Predictive Writing 119
1. Legal Memoranda.. 119
2. Incorporating Counter-Arguments.. 130
3. Checklist for Writing Legal Memoranda 132
4. Legal Advice via Email 135
5. Client or Opinion Letters 141
6. Bench Memoranda 146

Chapter 8. Legal Advocacy and Argument...................................... 155
1. How Does Advocacy Differ from Advice? 155
2. Appeals to *Pathos* in Legal Advocacy..................................... 156
3. Theory of the Case.. 158
4. Framing Your Client's Story 160
5. Framing the Law from Your Client's Perspective..................... 163
6. Appeals to *Ethos* in Legal Advocacy....................................... 166
7. A Lawyer's Duty of Candor to the Tribunal 168
8. Professionalism in Legal Advocacy 170

**Chapter 9. Arrangement in Legal Advocacy Related to
   Lawsuits** 173
1. Complaints.. 173
2. Motions... 179
3. Memoranda in Support of Motions... 182
4. Appellate Briefs... 188
5. What Is Standard of Review? 202
6. Drafting a Persuasive Statement of the Case 204
7. Organizing the Appellate Argument.. 206
8. Drafting Effective Headings and Roadmaps 212
9. Checklist for Writing Appellate Briefs 216

Chapter 10. Style.. 221
1. Legal Writing Style 221
2. Clear Legal Writing.. 224
3. Concise Legal Writing... 228
4. Legal Writing Conventions... 235
5. Proper Grammar, Usage, and Punctuation.............................. 239
6. Figures of Speech 247
7. Checklist for Style Issues... 251

Chapter 11. Memory and Delivery 255
1. Oral Reporting.. 255
2. Client Meetings 256
3. Oral Advocacy... 260

Appendix A. Print Version of *Copeland v. District of Columbia Department of Employment Services* 267

Appendix B. Sample Case Briefs of *Copeland v. District of Columbia Department of Employment Services* 275
Sample 1 275
Sample 2 276

Appendix C. Sample Legal Memorandum 277

Appendix D. Excerpts from Appellate Briefs in *Texas Beef Group v. Winfrey* 285
Excerpts from Appellant's Brief 285
Excerpts from Appellee's Brief 289

Appendix E. Bibliography 295
NAMES AND SUBJECTS INDEX 309

TABLE OF CONTENTS

PREFACE V

ACKNOWLEDGMENTS VII

Chapter 1. Introduction to Law School 1
1. Welcome to the Legal Profession 1
2. What Are Legal Research and Legal Writing? 2
3. How Does Legal Research and Writing Differ from Other First-Year Courses? 6
4. How Do You Read for Class? 7
   A. A Typical Judicial Decision 8
   B. How to Read and Brief Judicial Decisions 11
5. What Do Your Professors Expect of You? 13

Chapter 2. Law and Rhetoric 15
1. What Is Rhetoric? 15
2. A Brief History of Rhetoric 17
   A. Ancient Greece and Rome (c. 466 BCE–50 CE) 18
      i. The Greeks 19
      ii. The Romans 22
   B. The Second Sophists and Early Christianity (c. 50–400 CE) 24
   C. The Middle Ages (c. 500–1400 CE) 27
   D. The Renaissance (c. 1400–1600 CE) 28
   E. The Seventeenth and Eighteenth Centuries (c. 1600–1800 CE) 30
      i. The Early Epistemologists 31
      ii. The Eighteenth-Century Epistemologists 34
      iii. The Neo-Classicists 35
      iv. The Belletristic Scholars 35
   F. The Nineteenth Century 36
3. Why Don't Law Schools Teach Rhetoric? 36
4. Law as Rhetoric 39
5. Do Objective Rules of Law Exist Out There Somewhere? 41
   A. American Legal Realism 41
   B. Postmodern Theories of Law 42

Chapter 3. The Rhetorical Process 47
1. Aristotle's Canons of Rhetoric 47
2. What Is Writing, or How Were You Taught to Write? 49
   A. Theories of Writing 50
      i. Writing as the Expression of Knowledge or External Reality 50

       ii.   Writing as the Expression of Knowledge or Reality from
            Within the Writer 51
       iii.   Writing as a Process That Creates Knowledge or
            Constructs Reality 51
   B.   The Effect of Writing Theories on Legal Research and Writing
       Courses 53
3.   Take Time to Assess Your Research and Writing Persona 53
   A.   Research 54
   B.   Writing 54
       i.   Prewriting 55
       ii.   Writing 55

Chapter 4. Discovering Arguments 57
1.   Sources of Law 57
2.   Statutory Interpretation 58
   A.   The Format of a Typical Statute 58
   B.   Tools for Interpreting Statutes 59
3.   Hierarchy of Authority 61
   A.   Federal Courts 62
   B.   State Courts 62
   C.   *Stare Decisis* 63
4.   Print and Online Resources 65
   A.   The Old Days 66
   B.   Research Methods Today 67
   C.   Differences in Online Databases 67
       i.   Proprietary Databases 68
       ii.   Low-Cost 68
       iii.   Free 69
   D.   Using Print Versus Online Resources 69
5.   The Research Process 69
   A.   Identify the Issue 70
   B.   Consult the Topics (i.e., Do the Research) 72
6.   Organize and Analyze as You Go 75

Chapter 5. Appeals to Reason 79
1.   The Analytical Paradigm 79
2.   Induction (Rule Synthesis) 80
   A.   What Is Rule Synthesis? 81
   B.   Rule Synthesis in Law 82
   C.   Faulty Generalizations 86
3.   Deduction (Legal Syllogisms) 87
   A.   The Categorical Syllogism in Logic 88
   B.   The Legal Syllogism 92
4.   Fallacies in Deductive Reasoning 97
   A.   The Book Report (Both Premises Missing) 97
   B.   Fear of Commitment (Missing a Conclusion) 98
   C.   The Deceptive Hypothetical (Denying the Antecedent) 99

D.   The Double Negative Proof (Two No's Don't Make a Yes) 100
E.   Begging the Question 101
5.   A Modern Take on the Legal Syllogism 101
6.   Analogical Reasoning 103
7.   Fallacies in Analogical Reasoning 106
A.   The Missing Link (Too Much Missing Information) 106
B.   The House of Cards (Relying on a Case with an Adverse
     Outcome) 107
C.   The Problem with Totality of Circumstances Tests 108
8.   Narrative Reasoning 109
9.   Policy-Based Reasoning 111

Chapter 6. Legal Advice and Predictive Writing 115
1.   What Is Predictive Writing? 115
2.   Appeals to *Pathos* in Predictive Writing 116
3.   Appeals to *Ethos* in Predictive Writing 117

Chapter 7. Arrangement in Predictive Writing 119
1.   Legal Memoranda 119
A.   Format of a Legal Memorandum 119
B.   Sample Memorandum in the Starbucks Matter 121
C.   Organization of the Discussion Section 127
     i.   Large-Scale Organization 127
     ii.   Small-Scale Organization 128
2.   Incorporating Counter-Arguments 130
A.   Anticipating Counter-Arguments in Predictive Writing 131
B.   Minimizing Counter-Arguments in Persuasive Writing 132
3.   Checklist for Writing Legal Memoranda 132
4.   Legal Advice via Email 135
A.   Format of Legal Advice via Email 135
B.   Sample Email in the Starbucks Matter 137
5.   Client or Opinion Letters 141
A.   Format of a Client Letter 141
B.   Sample Client Letter in the Starbucks Matter 142
6.   Bench Memoranda 146
A.   Format of a Bench Memorandum 147
B.   Sample Bench Memorandum in the Starbucks Matter 149

Chapter 8. Legal Advocacy and Argument 155
1.   How Does Advocacy Differ from Advice? 155
2.   Appeals to *Pathos* in Legal Advocacy 156
3.   Theory of the Case 158
4.   Framing Your Client's Story 160
5.   Framing the Law from Your Client's Perspective 163
6.   Appeals to *Ethos* in Legal Advocacy 166
7.   A Lawyer's Duty of Candor to the Tribunal 168
8.   Professionalism in Legal Advocacy 170

Chapter 9. Arrangement in Legal Advocacy Related to Lawsuits 173

1. Complaints 173
   A. Format of a Complaint 173
   B. Sample Complaint in the Starbucks Matter 175
2. Motions 179
   A. Format of a Motion 179
   B. Sample Motion in the Starbucks Matter 181
3. Memoranda in Support of Motions 182
   A. Format of a Memorandum of Points and Authorities 182
   B. Sample Memorandum of Points and Authorities in the
      Starbucks Matter 183
4. Appellate Briefs 188
   A. Format of an Appellate Brief 189
   B. Sample Appellate Brief in the Starbucks Matter 192
   C. Sample Appellate Briefs on a Related Issue 202
5. What Is Standard of Review? 202
6. Drafting a Persuasive Statement of the Case 204
   A. Include the Introduction and Rising Action of Your Client's
      Story 205
   B. Specific Techniques for Drafting Persuasive Facts 205
7. Organizing the Appellate Argument 206
   A. Large-Scale Organization 206
   B. Small-Scale Organization of Individual Arguments 209
8. Drafting Effective Headings and Roadmaps 212
   A. Major, Minor, and Sub-Headings 212
   B. Use Roadmaps to Explain the Division of Your Argument into
      Various Headings 214
9. Checklist for Writing Appellate Briefs 216

Chapter 10. Style 221

1. Legal Writing Style 221
2. Clear Legal Writing 224
   A. Avoid Latin Words and Phrases 225
   B. Avoid Old-Fashioned Words and Phrases 226
   C. Avoid Redundancies 226
   D. Avoid Elegant Variation 227
   E. Use Passive Voice Intentionally and Selectively 227
   F. Avoid Double Negatives 228
3. Concise Legal Writing 228
   A. Avoid Long Sentences with Strings of Intrusive Clauses
      and Phrases 229
   B. Discuss Only Those Issues Relevant to Your Analysis 229
   C. Devote No More Space to an Issue than It Deserves 230
   D. State Elements of a Cause of Action or Crime Just Once 230
   E. Do Not Summarize the History of the Controlling Rules
      of Law 230

F. Do Not Explain to the Reader What You, as the Writer, Intend to Do or What You Are Thinking.. 230

G. You May Condense Your Analysis by Combining Topic Sentences with Predictions, Argument, or Rules of Law.............. 231

H. Omit Unnecessary Words and Phrases That Add No Meaning 232

I. Avoid Nominalizations 232

J. In Analogical Reasoning, Summarize Only the Facts, Issues, and Reasoning of the Cited Case(s) That Are Helpful to Your Analysis.. 233

K. Use Explanatory Parentheticals to Add Supporting Authority Without Adding Length 234

4. Legal Writing Conventions.. 235

A. Avoid Use of First Person in Formal Legal Writing 235

B. Do Not Use Contractions in Formal Legal Writing....................... 236

C. Spell Judgment with One "E" 236

D. Do Not Pose Questions to the Reader 236

E. Use Adverbs Sparingly.. 236

F. Use Few Direct Quotes.. 236

G. Use Past Tense to Discuss Cited Cases and Present Tense to Discuss Your Case 237

H. Spell Out the Word "Section" in Text.. 237

I. Use a Comma to Separate All Items in a Series 237

J. Use First, Not Firstly, in a List of Reasons 237

K. Refer to Corporations and Courts as "Its" 237

L. Avoid Proper Names When Describing Case Law 238

M. Capitalize "Court" Only When Referring to the United States Supreme Court or the Court You Are Addressing.......................... 238

N. You May Use Em Dashes to Set Off Important Phrases 238

O. Avoid Colloquialisms and Slang... 238

P. Numerals.. 238

Q. Use Proper Date Form 239

R. Use *Supra*, *Infra*, and *See Generally* Only for Secondary Materials 239

5. Proper Grammar, Usage, and Punctuation.. 239

A. Place Commas and Periods Inside Quotation Marks..................... 239

B. Place Colons and Semi-Colons Outside Quotation Marks............. 239

C. Place Question and Exclamation Marks Inside Quotation Marks Only if They Are Part of the Quotation.............................. 240

D. Quotations of Fifty or More Words Should Be Set Off as Block Quotes... 240

E. Use Commas After Introductory Phrases 241

F. Use Commas Between Independent Clauses Joined by Coordinating Conjunctions 241

G. Use Semi-Colons to Join Independent Clauses That Are Related in Some Way 241

H. Use Semi-Colons to Separate Items in a Series, Where Any Item of the Series Contains a Comma 242

I.   Use Hyphens to Join Compound Adjectives 242
J.   Avoid Splitting Infinitives... 242
K.   Use "That" and "Which" Correctly; If in Doubt, Use "That" 242
L.   Use Correct Plural Forms for Singular Words Ending in "S" 243
M.   Use Correct Possessive Forms for Words Ending in "S" 243
N.   Avoid Pronouns with Ambiguous Referents 243
O.   Make Sure Nouns/Verbs and Nouns/Pronouns Agree 244
P.   Do Not End Sentences with Prepositions 244
Q.   Avoid Dangling Modifiers 245
R.   Place "Only" as Close as Possible to the Word or Phrase It
     Modifies 245
S.   Use "Hopefully" and "Badly" Properly 245
T.   Commonly Confused Words 246
6.   Figures of Speech 247
A.   Alliteration.. 247
B.   Assonance... 247
C.   Irony 248
D.   Metaphor.. 248
E.   Onomatopoeia 250
F.   Oxymoron 250
G.   Paradox 250
H.   Personification 250
I.   Simile.. 250
7.   Checklist for Style Issues... 251

Chapter 11. Memory and Delivery 255
1.   Oral Reporting... 255
2.   Client Meetings 256
3.   Oral Advocacy 260
A.   Typical Oral Argument 260
B.   Oral Argument Etiquette 264
C.   How to Prepare for Oral Argument... 265

**Appendix A. Print Version of *Copeland v. District of Columbia
Department of Employment Services***.. 267

**Appendix B. Sample Case Briefs of *Copeland v. District of
Columbia Department of Employment Services***.............................. 275
Sample 1 275
Sample 2 276

Appendix C. Sample Legal Memorandum 277

**Appendix D. Excerpts from Appellate Briefs in *Texas Beef Group
v. Winfrey***.. 285
Excerpts from Appellant's Brief.. 285
Excerpts from Appellee's Brief... 289

Appendix E. Bibliography 295

NAMES AND SUBJECTS INDEX.. 309

RHETORIC FOR LEGAL WRITERS

THE THEORY AND PRACTICE OF ANALYSIS AND PERSUASION

Second Edition

CHAPTER 1

INTRODUCTION TO LAW SCHOOL

∎ ∎ ∎

1. WELCOME TO THE LEGAL PROFESSION

A well-functioning society needs lawyers. We especially need lawyers who can write well. Practicing law can take many different forms: prosecuting or defending an accused criminal in court, drafting legislation, advising a business how to comply with federal and state regulations, negotiating a merger between two companies, or mediating a divorce settlement, to name a few. Each of these activities requires that the lawyer know how to research, reason, speak, and write well in order to achieve her client's goals. These skills often distinguish the great lawyer from the good one.

Whether or not you choose to practice law, your legal education will change you. You will never look the same way again at an apartment lease, an airplane ticket, a loan instrument, or a set of terms and conditions on the internet. You will feel like a whole new world has opened up to you, with its own, complicated language. Learning this language is exciting. Most first-year law students soon find themselves talking about the law constantly, even at parties. You may find yourself becoming impatient with family and friends who are not immersed in the same, intensive law school experience because they do not understand what you are going through. In the end, you will come to appreciate how deeply the law influences our daily lives.

Regardless of where and why you are attending law school, you will undoubtedly learn to think differently and more analytically—like a lawyer. Thinking like a lawyer starts with a client: an individual, a corporation, or some other business entity or organization with a legal problem and a story to tell. To think like a lawyer is to begin solving the problem by asking questions, enlisting the client's help to collect all pertinent facts, and reserving judgment. With perhaps a sense of the applicable legal principles, the lawyer conducts thorough and efficient research to learn the controlling law and apply it to the legally significant facts. Based on the client's needs, she will then be in a position to explain the law and predict, negotiate, or argue for a particular outcome.

The point of law school is to teach you this essential and unique skill set. You will learn rules of law that come from constitutions, statutes, and judicial decisions on a variety of subject matters ranging from property to tax to criminal law. But law school is less about this "black letter" law than the ability to find, read, interpret, shape, and apply it in the service of your clients' goals. In that sense, it's more about the rhetoric of law than the law itself. And this book will introduce you to the core concepts of rhetoric. Often, people find the reference to "rhetoric" in this context off-putting. Since the time of Plato, rhetoric has been considered by some as inferior to philosophy and science. In ancient Greece, a teacher of rhetoric was known as a sophist, which translates into a teacher of knowledge. But over time, the sophists' clever and ornate speech earned them a reputation for being manipulative. It was not a large leap to begin thinking of lawyers as masters of sophistry.[1]

Despite this negative connotation, rhetoric is a rich and diverse subject. Today, it is the study of all human communication, including persuasion. It is a method for learning how to communicate effectively and for interpreting and analyzing language. As you will read, it was used for thousands of years to teach some of the greatest legal minds dating back to the ancient world. And it will inform everything you do in law school.

2. WHAT ARE LEGAL RESEARCH AND LEGAL WRITING?

The purpose of **legal research** is to find the law you need to help your client. It is both something you do and something you find.

You are already familiar with basic research techniques in print and online sources, but legal research is likely to seem very different. First, the sheer volume of law (that grows daily) makes it difficult to be sure you have found everything that is necessary or helpful to answer your questions. Second, there are multiple methods of research that can take you in circles, making it hard to know when to stop. Sometimes you stop simply because you run out of time. Third, and this may be new for you, you will need to become aware of the costs associated with research. Some online legal resources are very expensive, some have moderate costs, and some are free. If you have access to a good law library, print resources are almost always free. You will want to develop a technique that is cost effective both for your client and your practice. That means you will

---

[1]   Unfortunately, a generalized dislike of lawyers continued to permeate Western culture. *See, e.g.,* CHAUCER, *Prologue,* in CANTERBURY TALES, ll. 323–24 ("Nowhere a man so busy of his class, and yet he seemed much busier than he was."); JOYCE CAROL OATES, RAPE: A LOVE STORY 70 (2003) ("A lawyer is basically a mouth, like a shark is a mouth attached to a long gut. The business of lawyers is to talk, to interrupt one another, and to devour one another if possible."); WILL ROGERS, *The Lawyers Talking, in* 6 WILL ROGERS' WEEKLY ARTICLES: THE ROOSEVELT YEARS, 1933–1935, at 208 (Steven K. Gragert ed., Will Rogers Mem'l Museums rev. ed. 2011) (1982), http://www.willrogers.com/papers/weekly/WA-Vol-6.pdf ("The minute you read something and you can't understand it you can almost be sure that it was drawn up by a lawyer."); WILLIAM SHAKESPEARE, THE SECOND PART OF KING HENRY VI act 4, sc. 2 ("The first thing we do, let's kill all the lawyers.").

situation and giving advice, it helps to keep your clients' goals in mind. As you will learn later in law school, you have an ethical duty to represent your clients zealously, but you must be respectful too. Always assume your clients are being truthful, be careful how you characterize facts in writing, and never use sarcasm or irony because it does not transfer well to writing. Try to propose various options as neutrally as possible, being careful to identify the advantages and disadvantages of each. Finally, be honest with respect to your clients' ability to achieve their goals.

In the Starbucks case, for example, you would assume at the outset that the beans are indeed organic and that the owner has lost money in sales (proof of that can come a bit later). You would never want to suggest that the owner is somehow not worthy of or in need of compensation. You wouldn't say, for example, "Given how successful Starbucks is, I assume any losses can be absorbed by the company. Nevertheless, if you feel you must recover them, I recommend the following: . . ." That kind of language is sure to offend your client and makes too many assumptions about the facts. Nor would you conclude that "of all the options, I like the second one best" without explaining why it is preferable as a legal matter. Otherwise, you run the risk of unduly influencing your client's ultimate decision.

3. APPEALS TO *ETHOS* IN PREDICTIVE WRITING

"For the man who seems bad when he speaks must inevitably speak badly."

—Quintilian

Ethical appeals demonstrate a speaker's credibility. According to Aristotle, a speaker must have a good character and be credible: "He must give the right impression of himself, and get his judge into the right state of mind."[5] Cicero said that speakers should make their audience "well-disposed, attentive, and receptive."[6] Quintilian developed an even broader view of appeals to ethos. He defined "a good man skilled in speaking" as a person free from vice, a lover of wisdom, a sincere believer in his cause, and a servant of the people.[7]

Aristotle said that a speaker cannot persuade unless the audience likes and respects him. The same holds true for legal writing. The reader must believe your writing is genuine and credible. Just as inaccuracy and exaggeration can offend your reader, they can cause readers to lose faith in your credibility. For that reason, do not assume, speculate about, or exaggerate facts.

---

[5]   ARISTOTLE, RHETORIC, *supra* ch. 2, note 2, at bk. 2, ch. 1, p. 91.

[6]   2 CICERO, DE INVENTIONE, *supra* ch. 2, note 26, bk. 1, ch. 15, ¶ 20, p. 41.

[7]   QUINTILIAN, INSTITUTIO ORATORIO, ch. 2, *supra* note 32, at bk. 12, ch. 1, pp. 197–203.

To synthesize reasonable rules of law, you need to conduct thorough research (including updating). Because legal readers are doubting readers, you will need to cite adequate supporting authority to prove that the law is what you say it is and formulate reasonable rules (i.e., demonstrate that your major premises are at least probably true). As you will learn in a course on professional responsibility, you also have an ethical obligation to disclose to your client (and any ultimate decision maker) any binding authority that refutes or is inconsistent with your client's position.[8] Open and honest disclosure serves to increase your credibility.

Credibility in legal writing depends on:

- an accurate and fair characterization of the facts
- thorough legal research
- citation to adequate supporting authority
- reasonable, synthesized rules of law
- disclosure of binding negative authority
- a professional-looking product

Finally, your first chance to make a good impression with your writing is the physical appearance of the document itself. It's like the icing on a cake because it is the first thing the reader sees. If your writing looks sloppy, is full of errors, or fails to conform to applicable rules (agency, court, or customary), the reader will suspect there is something wrong with the cake too. For more on professionalism in legal writing, see Chapter 8.8.

---

8   MODEL RULES OF PROF'L CONDUCT r. 3.3(a)(2) (Am. Bar Ass'n 2015).

CHAPTER 7

ARRANGEMENT IN PREDICTIVE WRITING

■ ■ ■

1. LEGAL MEMORANDA

Legal memoranda are used to inform the client about the law, predict outcome, and determine next steps. They can be written for clients (especially when the client is another lawyer), other lawyers working for the same client, or even "the client file" to preserve the lawyer's thought process. Before fax machines, the internet, or PDFs, the legal memorandum was a primary form of communication between lawyers and clients. Today, the legal profession moves at a faster pace, and clients may prefer getting some or all of their advice via email (see Chapter 7.4). Nevertheless, there will be many occasions when a traditional, comprehensive memorandum is necessary or appropriate.

A. FORMAT OF A LEGAL MEMORANDUM

The traditional legal memorandum is organized like a classical speech in that it is

> a progression of steps that begins with an [introduction] designed to secure the goodwill of one's audience, next states one's own position, then points up the nature of the dispute, then builds up one's own case at length, then refutes the claims of the adversary, and in a final [conclusion] expands and reinforces all points in one's favor, while seeking to discredit whatever had favored the adversary.[1]

A sample memorandum in the Starbucks case appears on pp. 121–127.

Heading

The heading indicates to whom the memo is written, by whom, for what purpose, and when.

Question Presented

The question presented is a statement of the legal question(s) to be resolved. It should include the controlling (binding or mandatory) jurisdiction or law, the specific legal question, and a pithy statement of the legally significant facts. There is no one format for drafting Questions Presented as long as they contain this information. Typical forms include:

---

[1]   KENNETH BURKE, A RHETORIC OF MOTIVES 69 (1950).

"Under [applicable federal or state law], can the client recover for [cause of action], given [these particular facts]?"

"Whether the client can recover for [cause of action] under [applicable federal or state law] given [these particular facts]."

A question presented that begins with "whether" usually ends with a period, rather than a question mark.

Brief Answer

A brief answer summarizes the lawyer's answer to the legal question. Typically, it begins with a one or two-word answer like "probably not," "unlikely," or "no," and then proceeds in a paragraph or two to summarize the legal analysis. A good Brief Answer includes the legal framework for answering the question presented (e.g., the elements of a false disparagement claim), the ultimate conclusion on the application of each of those rules, and the writer's reasoning. No citations are required. Even the doubting legal reader will wait for proof (i.e., citations) until the discussion section.

Statement of Facts

The statement of facts includes the client's story to date, the client's goals, and any relevant procedural history. The story should include all legally significant facts and any other background facts necessary to put the story in context. The procedural history can come at the beginning or end. Because it is not always easy to identify the legally significant facts, some legal writers prefer to write the facts section after they write the discussion. Any facts used in the discussion should appear in the statement of facts so as not to confuse or surprise the reader. Once you present the client's full story in this section, it can easily be referred to in other parts of the memorandum.

Discussion

The discussion sets forth the detailed analysis of each issue, including citations to authority. Typically, a discussion begins with an introductory paragraph or two (often referred to as a "**roadmap**" for the reader of your analysis) that sets forth the framework of the law to be analyzed. The Romans called this the outline of the arguments. As Cicero explained, it helps the reader "hold definite points in his mind, and to understand that when these have been discussed the [analysis] will be over."[2]

The discussion then analyzes each issue in turn in a systematic and logical way. Your analysis should be organized according to the rules of law in the order you referred to them in the roadmap (see detailed discussion on organization below).

---

[2]   2 CICERO, DE INVENTIONE, *supra* ch. 2, note 26, bk. 1, ch. 22, ¶ 31, p. 63.

Conclusion

The conclusion summarizes the writer's analysis in more detail than the brief answer. It acts to recap the discussion section and reinforce it in the reader's mind. The length of the conclusion varies depending on the complexity of the analysis but one to two pages at most is common. As with brief answers, citations are not required.

B. SAMPLE MEMORANDUM IN THE STARBUCKS MATTER

To: Supervising Attorney

From: Junior Associate

Date: July 1, 2015

Re: Ramon Velas/false disparagement

Question Presented

Under Texas statutory law, can Ramon Velas, doing business as Starbucks, recover against Citizens for Safe Products (CSP) for false disparagement when CSP published statements in its monthly newsletter claiming that Starbucks' coffee beans are grown using pesticides?

This Question Presented identifies the controlling law, legal issue, and legally significant facts.

Brief Answer

Probably yes, as to coffee beans but not coffee drinks. In order to succeed in a claim for false disparagement under the Texas statute, Starbucks must prove three elements. First, Starbucks must prove that CSP disseminated information in any manner to the public about a "perishable food product." Although CSP likely disseminated information about a perishable food product to the public through its newsletter, the product is likely limited to coffee beans. Perishable food products are sole, as opposed to combined, products of agriculture or aquaculture, and thus prepared coffee drinks do not qualify for protection. Second, CSP likely knew its information was false. Because it does not appear to have contacted Starbucks or its suppliers about

This Brief Answer includes the legal framework for answering the Question Presented (e.g., the elements of a false disparagement claim and the producer requirement), the ultimate answer to the question (e.g., the prediction as to each element and whether Starbucks is a producer), and the writer's reasoning.

the truth of its statements, it demonstrated a reckless indifference to the truth that likely equates to actual knowledge. Third, the information implied that Starbucks' beans are unsafe for consumption by the public by associating them with pesticides. Starbucks must also prove that it is a producer of a perishable food product. Although Starbucks does not grow the beans, which are roasted before Starbucks imports them from outside Texas, the statute appears to protect unprocessed and processed food products sold, not necessarily grown, in Texas.

Statement of Facts

Our client is Ramon Velas, doing business as Starbucks, who owns a coffee shop in Dallas, Texas. Velas attributes part of his success to selling and using only organically grown coffee beans from fair trade sources. CSP is a California non-profit corporation, with a local Dallas chapter comprised of about fifty members. It publishes a monthly newsletter about products sold in the Dallas area. In March 2015, CSP published a newsletter stating that Starbucks' beans are grown using pesticides. Immediately after the newsletter was distributed, Starbucks' coffee bean and drink sales dropped significantly, which Mr. Velas attributes to the statements in the newsletter. He has had to dispose of hundreds of packages of whole and ground beans that did not sell by their "best before" dates, which range from six to eight weeks from the time of production. To his knowledge, CSP made no effort to contact him or Starbucks Coffee Company to verify the statements in its newsletter before it was distributed. Mr. Velas is interested in recovering lost sales from CSP. This memo addresses the likelihood of success under just one of several potential claims.[3]

The Statement of Facts identifies the parties, sets forth the background as well as legally significant facts, and states the client's goal.

---

[3]   The extra spaces between paragraphs in the text of the memorandum are to make room for the annotations at right.

Discussion

Mr. Velas is likely to succeed in an action against CSP for false disparagement with respect to losses in coffee bean sales but not coffee drinks. Section 96.002 of the Texas false disparagement statute makes a person liable to the producer of a perishable food product if

> (a) the person disseminates in any manner information relating to a perishable food product to the public;

> (b) the person knows the information is false; and

> (c) the information states or implies that the perishable food product is not safe for consumption by the public.

Tex. Civ. Prac. & Rem. Code Ann. § 96.002 (Vernon 2011).

The first element (a) requires Velas to prove that CSP disseminated information in any manner to the public and that coffee is a perishable food product. *See* § 96.002(a). The information must be disseminated to a large enough audience to constitute the "public" in the ordinary sense of the word. *Green's Grocer v. Janus*, 228 S.W.2d 94, 95 (Tex. 2012). In *Green's Grocer*, the defendant disseminated information to the public when he made his statement on a local TV news broadcast, presumably because the court assumed a large number of viewers watched the broadcast. *Id.* Here, the consumer group sent its newsletter by email to fifty subscribers, which is also a large number of people. Just as the broadcast was heard by a large number of viewers, the email was received by a large number of subscribers. Although the court did not articulate the number of viewers or readers necessary to be large enough, fifty is likely enough to constitute the "public" in the ordinary sense of the word.

The first paragraph of the Discussion introduces the reader to the legal framework for a cause of action for false disparagement by listing its required elements. By stating each of the elements in order, it creates a natural outline or roadmap for the Discussion and reader to follow.

The topic sentence here indicates that the writer is going to discuss the first element in this paragraph.

Notice that this element has two discrete sub-issues, which the writer will address separately and in order. After the topic sentence, the writer states a synthesized rule from *Green's Grocer* on dissemination to "the public" (the major premise) and explains the rule by discussing the facts, holding, and reasoning in that case.

Next, the writer describes Velas' situation (the minor premise), compares it to *Green's Grocer* (by analogy), and concludes that the court would rule similarly in his case on this aspect of the first element (i.e., there was dissemination to the public).

Velas must also prove that coffee (either beans or drinks) is a perishable food product. The statute does not define food product, but "food" is generally understood to mean a nutritious substance ingested to maintain health and life. *See, e.g.,* OXFORD ENGLISH DICTIONARY 279 (7th ed. 2012). Even though we do not think of coffee as food, coffee beans contain nutrients such as potassium and magnesium as well as antioxidants. Since coffee is often combined with other ingredients that contain calories, such as sugar, milk, syrup, etc. and ingested, it may qualify as food under the statute.

This paragraph discusses whether coffee is a food product as part of the second sub-issue of the first element. Since there is no controlling law, the writer uses plain meaning and the dictionary to form the major premise.

The minor premise consists of the general make-up of coffee beans.

A perishable food product is "a food product of agriculture or aquaculture that is sold or distributed in a form that will perish or decay beyond marketability within a limited period of time." § 96.001. To qualify, the product must be a sole food product, not a combination of products, and "a limited period of time" may mean no more than six months. *The Pet Barn, Inc. v. Holmes*, 224 S.W.2d 99, 102 (Tex. 2004). In *Pet Barn*, the court held that a baked pet snack was not a product of agriculture even though it contained products of agriculture: "The result is a *combination* of products of agriculture, not a sole product of agriculture as the statute contemplates." *Id.* Under this definition, coffee beans could be perishable food products but not coffee drinks. Like baked pet snacks, most Starbucks coffee drinks are a combination of products of agriculture such as sugar and milk. They also contain water. We might try to distinguish *Pet Barn* on the ground that coffee drinks are different because the agricultural ingredients are not chemically altered by baking as they were in that case. However, this argument seems weak; it would extend protection under the statute to more plaintiffs and products than the legislature likely intended. For that reason, only Starbucks coffee beans likely qualify as perishable food products.

This paragraph discusses whether coffee is perishable. The major premise comes from the definition in the statute. The synthesized rule on what a product of agriculture is comes from *Pet Barn*.

Here, the writer explains the stated rule by discussing the *Pet Barn* case, including key facts, holding, and reasoning.

Here, the writer applies the rule on "product of agriculture" to the facts and, in the process, distinguishes *Pet Barn* with respect to coffee beans but not drinks. The writer includes a policy-based reason why coffee drinks likely do not qualify for protection.

The beans must also "perish or decay" beyond marketability within a limited period of time. The statute does not define "limited period of time," but since it is designed to protect sellers of meat, fish, and produce, it likely refers to days or weeks as opposed to several months. The court in *Pet Barn* indicated that six months is likely not a limited period. *Id.* at 102. Although coffee beans do not perish or decay in days or weeks, they do have a "best before" date of six to eight weeks, far less than six months, past which Velas will no longer sell them because they begin to lose flavor. For that reason, they likely perish or decay beyond marketability within a limited period of time.

> This paragraph completes the discussion of the second sub-issue. In the absence of controlling law, the synthesized rule on what a limited period of time means is based on plain meaning and common sense.

The second element (b) requires that Velas prove that CSP knew the information it disseminated was false. Knowledge of falsity can include actual knowledge as well as a reckless indifference to truth. *Thomas Meats v. Safeway*, 10 S.W.3d 45 (Tex. 2007). In *Thomas Meats*, the defendant grocery store posted a sign in its windows saying that the plaintiff's meats were unsafe. Because the defendant had relied solely on rumors and failed to investigate the truth of those rumors, the court held the store's "reckless indifference to the truth was tantamount to knowledge of falsity." *Id.* at 46. Although we have no information indicating that CSP had actual knowledge of falsity, it failed to contact Velas, his suppliers, or Starbucks in general much as the store in *Thomas Meats* failed to investigate rumors about the meat the plaintiff was selling. Thus, a court is likely to find CSP's reckless indifference to the truth amounted to knowledge of falsity.

> This sentence makes it clear that this paragraph discusses the second element of a false disparagement claim.
>
> The synthesized rule follows the topic sentence.
>
> Conclusion on the second element.
>
> Explanation of rule.
>
> Comparison of CSP to store in *Thomas Meats*.

Velas is also likely to prove the third element (c) requiring that CSP stated or implied that coffee drinks are not safe for consumption by the public. To state or imply that a perishable food product is unsafe, the defendant must indicate that the product is inherently dangerous in some way. *Green's Grocer*, 228 S.W.2d at 95. There, the court held that a statement that a customer had choked on one of the plaintiff's apples did not imply that it was inherently dangerous because people choke on all sorts of food. *Id.* at 96.

> The topic sentence here introduces the discussion on the third element. Unlike in the preceding discussion, it also includes the writer's conclusion on this element. Either approach is generally acceptable, but be consistent throughout.

Unlike in *Green's Grocer*, CSP implied that the coffee beans are inherently dangerous. By saying the beans are grown using pesticides, CSP raised serious concern among consumers about the beans' safety. For years, the public has assumed pesticides and other chemicals used to grow crops can be carcinogenic or otherwise harmful. CSP might argue it stated only that the beans are not as advertised, but given the fears associated with chemicals in our food supply, Velas probably has the better argument.

Since *Green's Grocer* held for the defendant, the writer distinguishes it.

Finally, Velas must be a producer of the perishable food product to recover under the statute. § 96.002(b). Unlike other states, Texas does not limit the meaning of producer to those who actually farm or grow crops. *See, e.g.,* Fla. Stat. § 865.065 (2014) (limiting recovery to "the person who actually grows or produces" the food products). The legislative history also indicates that "unprocessed" was deleted from the definition of perishable food product "so the statute would apply to both processed and unprocessed food." H. Bill Analysis, 74–722, Reg. Sess., at 4 (Tex. 1995).

Conclusion on the third element.

Use of legislative history to interpret ambiguous term.

CSP might argue that the statute is intended to protect Texas farmers, not companies that resell imported agricultural products. However, since false statements about coffee beans have affected Velas' Starbucks in Texas, a court is likely to find that Velas is the producer of a food product for purposes of the Texas statute. Thus the fact that the beans are roasted and imported from outside Texas (i.e., processed) does not appear to disqualify Starbucks from being a producer.

Writer anticipates counter-argument and then concludes.

Conclusion

Velas may succeed in a false disparagement action against CSP with respect to its coffee beans but not its coffee drinks. As required by the Texas statute, he is likely to prove that CSP disseminated information regarding a perishable food product to the public. By sending its newsletter to fifty subscribers, CSP likely disseminated information to a large enough

The Conclusion summarizes the Discussion in more detail than the Brief Answer. It also presumes the reader's familiarity with the Discussion.

audience to constitute the public. The information was likely about a food product, since coffee beans are a sole agricultural product with some nutritious value that perish or decay beyond marketability within a limited time because the beans lose flavor in six to eight weeks.

Assuming that CSP did not contact Velas, his suppliers, or Starbucks about the truth of the statements in its newsletter, Velas is likely to prove the second element, which requires that CSP knew the information was false. This failure demonstrates a reckless indifference to truth that is equivalent to actual knowledge of falsity. Finally, Velas is likely to prove that CSP's newsletter implied that its beans are unsafe for consumption by the public. Most consumers associate pesticides with a health risk and would infer that the beans are inherently dangerous in some way.

Finally, Velas is likely a producer under the statute. The statute does not require that he actually grew the beans, and it protects both processed and unprocessed foods.

C. ORGANIZATION OF THE DISCUSSION SECTION

The discussion of each issue should mirror the **analytical paradigm** (see Chapter 5.1, p. 79), moving from general rules of law, including analogical reasoning where helpful or necessary, to specific conclusions. At the outset, consider both large- and small-scale organization, preferably in that order.

i. Large-Scale Organization

Once your arguments are "invented," they need to be arranged. For the most part, legal readers expect your analysis to proceed in a deductive manner. For **large-scale organization**, use the roadmap to lay out the framework of the law, then organize your analysis first by issue and then by the general rules of law that apply to that issue. At first you may be tempted to or unconsciously organize your analysis around the cases you plan to discuss. This prevents you from reasoning deductively and synthesizing rules that reflect the current law. It may also cause you to repeat or contradict yourself. Moving from case to case also puts an undue burden on the reader to figure out what they mean and how they work together.

Large-Scale Organization

- organize first by issue and then by general rules of law (e.g., elements, factors, tests, etc.), NOT by cases

- begin with an introduction that outlines the analysis to follow

- address each issue (or sub-issue or combined issues) in turn, moving from general rules to specific conclusions

- use headings where helpful to visually divide analysis

- citations belong in text

As you systematically address each issue (and any sub-issues), do so in the order you laid them out in your roadmap (so you don't confuse your reader). State the general requirement or rule of law, provide a synthesized rule that explains what the rule means or how it has been interpreted (where necessary), apply the rule of law to the facts, consider any credible counter-arguments (see below) and make conclusions (i.e., predictions) as to each. At times, it may make sense to combine smaller, related issues. You may also want to use headings to make your organization clear to the reader. Typically, citations to authority are included in the text, not in footnotes.

For example, in the Starbucks case, the sole issue is whether Starbucks would succeed in a claim for false disparagement. The discussion in the sample memorandum on page 123 begins with a roadmap of the analysis to follow, explaining the three elements Starbucks must prove under the Texas statute. It then proceeds to address each element of the statute in turn, using syllogistic and analogical reasoning to apply the synthesized rules of law and conclude as to each element.

ii. Small-Scale Organization

The **small-scale organization** of each legal issue often mirrors that of the legal syllogism, but your analysis should contain more than two premises and a conclusion. Nor does each part of a legal syllogism need to be expressed in one sentence. Some issues take few sentences and one paragraph to analyze, while others take several sentences and several paragraphs. This small-scale organizational approach represents the deductive reasoning *process*. It is not a template for paragraphs.

As a matter of good writing, use topic sentences to identify each time you begin the discussion of a new issue or sub-issue. Some lawyers simply identify the issue; others identify the issue and state their ultimate conclusion on that issue. Ask your professor or colleagues if they have a preference (see the sample memorandum on p. 121).

Then, state the general requirement or rule of law (often accompanied by a synthesized rule to further explain its meaning) and cite binding or persuasive authority. Use cites from the most recent cases from the supreme or appellate courts in your jurisdiction because they are current statements of binding authority (see "the bull's-eye," Chapter 4.5, p. 72). The cases you cite in support of the rule need not be factually similar to your case.

Next, it is usually helpful to explain how the stated rule was applied in a similar case, how the court ruled, and why, including citations. This may or may not be the same case you cite in support of the general rule of law. If the case you cite can do double duty, it will make your writing more concise. Then apply the rule of law to your client's facts, making analogies to similar cases where possible.

Before concluding, you will need to consider any vulnerability in your "objective analysis." This is often referred to as anticipating the **counter-arguments** an opponent might make. For a complete discussion of counter-arguments, see the next section.

Remember that different legal issues and factual circumstances will call for different amounts and types of

---

Small-Scale Organization

For each issue or combined issues, include

- a topic sentence that identifies the issue (and perhaps states your prediction on that issue)

- the general requirement or rule (usually accompanied by a synthesized rule that explains what the rule means or how it has been interpreted) and citation to authority **[major premise]**

- if helpful and available, an explanation of the rule and how it was applied in a similar context

- application of the rule of law to the client's facts using analogies to prior binding cases **[minor premise]**

- potential counter-arguments

- a prediction **[conclusion]**

Remember: This approach represents an analytical process, not a template for paragraphs.

---

legal authority, discussion, and detail. That means some issues will require that you cite one or more statutory provisions, cite one or more cases or other sources of law, analogize or distinguish several cases, or take several paragraphs to analyze fully. That's okay. At other times, you may not have any helpful cases to analogize or distinguish. Even then, however, frame your analysis deductively to increase its effectiveness.

Attached at Appendix C is a student-written, sample memorandum on an issue of tort law. The question presented is whether an employee has a cause of action for retaliatory discharge under the Michigan

Whistleblower Protection Act. The annotations demonstrate how the theory described here is applied.

2. INCORPORATING COUNTER-ARGUMENTS

In both predictive and persuasive writing, you will need to anticipate what your client's opponent will argue: in order to predict outcome, you need to assess the strength of the opponent's position, and in order to persuade, you need to convince the decision-maker why your arguments are better.

Counter-arguments include:

- denials of a party's allegations (usually a factual dispute)

- disagreement with the party's characterization of the controlling law

- a superseding law or circumstance that affects the outcome despite the party's arguments (usually an affirmative defense)

There are several types of counter-arguments. The first is the **denial of a party's allegations**. Assume the plaintiff in a car accident case alleges that the light was red when the defendant drove through an intersection as she crossed the street in front of him. If the circumstances allow, you might anticipate the defendant claiming the light was green. Denials of allegations can involve questions of fact, questions of law, or mixed questions of law and fact.

For example, in the Starbucks case, Velas must allege that CSP knowingly disseminated false information to the public about a perishable food product that stated or implied his coffee is unsafe. CSP is likely to deny all of these allegations: the information was not false, it was not disseminated to the public, CSP had no knowledge of falsity, the information did not involve a "perishable food product," and the information did not state or imply the coffee was unsafe for consumption.

A second type of counter-argument is a **disagreement with the party's characterization of the controlling law**. The opponent may argue that your interpretation of the law is incorrect, overbroad, or too narrow. Or that the law has been modified in some way. For example, you might interpret the terms of a statute to mean one thing and expect your opponent to argue the terms mean something else (e.g., "producer" of a "perishable food product"). You might interpret a case to stand for a certain proposition of law and then expect your opponent to claim you have read the case too narrowly. Or your opponent may claim the holding of the case you rely on has been modified by the holding of a later case from the same jurisdiction.

For example, in the sample legal memorandum in the Starbucks case (Chapter 7.1, p. 121), the writer relies on *Green's Grocer* to argue that CSP disseminated information to the public. In that case, the court held that information is disseminated to the public if disseminated to "a large enough audience" to constitute the public "in the sense we normally mean that word." The writer then anticipates that CSP will claim *Green's Grocer* is distinguishable because the statement was made on local television news, which has a much larger audience than the fifty subscribers to whom it sent the March 2015 newsletter. In effect, CSP would be arguing that Velas has read *Green's Grocer* too broadly.

A third type of counter-argument is the **superseding argument**. It is the argument that even if your allegations are true, or your interpretation of the law is correct, there is another controlling law that supersedes or "trumps" yours. For example, assume the defendant in the car accident case claimed even if the light was red as he approached the intersection, he attempted to stop and avoid hitting the pedestrian, but his brakes failed. Having no knowledge that the brakes were faulty, his liability may be negated, at least in part. Here, the fact that the defendant had no knowledge that his brakes were about to fail might supersede or "trump" (in part) the fact that the light was red and he was required to stop.

As in the example above, superseding arguments are often **affirmative defenses** that excuse or limit the defendant's liability in a civil or criminal context. Typical affirmative defenses in a civil context include contributory negligence, assumption of the risk, consent, and even statutes of limitation, which prevent liability if the plaintiff fails to assert its rights after a certain period of time has elapsed. Insanity, necessity, and self-defense are a few examples of affirmative defenses in a criminal context.

A. ANTICIPATING COUNTER-ARGUMENTS IN PREDICTIVE WRITING

In predictive writing, the strength of your analysis rests heavily on your ability to anticipate the best arguments your client's opponent will make. To do that, put yourself in the shoes of the opponent. How would *you* respond to your analysis? What factual allegations would you deny? Which interpretations of the law would you challenge? Would you rely on different law? Are there any rules of law or cases that might act to negate your legal arguments?

You need not raise and then resolve each counter-argument an opponent could conceivably make. If the argument is unsupportable, it is probably not worth your time or the client's money. As a rule of thumb, raise and grapple with those counter-arguments you think legitimately challenge your analysis and could affect the ultimate outcome. If there is a case with an unfavorable outcome that you can expect the opponent to rely on and that does not fit well within the pattern of cases on the issue, it is probably worth discussing.

B. MINIMIZING COUNTER-ARGUMENTS IN PERSUASIVE WRITING

In persuasive writing, advocates should anticipate their opponent's counter-arguments and refute them. The goal is to persuade the decision-maker that you have already factored these arguments into your argument, and they do not present a problem for your client. But there is a fine line between needing to anticipate a credible counter-argument and not making your opponent's best arguments. In legal advocacy, be even more judicious about the counter-arguments you raise; address only those that present significant problems for your client. If your client's opponent raises a counter-argument you did not anticipate or chose not to address, you will usually have at least one opportunity to respond to it in writing (usually in the form of a reply brief).

For an example of how to anticipate counter-arguments in an appellate brief, see Chapter 9.4, pp. 197–200.

3. CHECKLIST FOR WRITING LEGAL MEMORANDA

You may find this checklist helpful in assessing a legal memorandum you are working on:

Question Presented (p. 119)

Includes:

- Controlling authority/jurisdiction
- Specific legal question
- Significant facts

Uses "Under, can, given," "Whether," or a complete sentence to state the question at issue.

Brief Answer (p. 120)

Summarizes the applicable legal rules and analysis in your own words, including why or how you reached a particular conclusion.

May combine rules and analysis to make writing concise: (e.g., topic sentence: Velas will be able to prove the first element because . . .).

Does not include citations to authority.

Statement of Facts (p. 120)

Contains the complete story on which the analysis is based: background, emotional, and legally significant facts. Contains all facts referred to in the discussion section.

Discussion (p. 120)

Content:

- Synthesizes all relevant and applicable constitutional, statutory, administrative, and common law. Is anything missing?

- Sets forth an outline for analysis in a roadmap/introductory paragraph.

- Analyzes each element, factor, requirement, etc. in a deductive manner: general rule (e.g. the product must perish or decay in a limited period of time), synthesized rule if necessary or helpful (e.g. six to eight weeks may qualify but six months does not), application of rule, and conclusion.

- Uses case analogies where helpful and available and distinguishes problematic case law.

- Addresses the opponent's best counter-arguments (p. 130).

- Reaches an ultimate conclusion on each disputed issue in a way that is consistent with the Brief Answer (p. 120).

Organization

Large Scale: (p. 127)

- Is organized first by issue and then by general requirements or rules of law (e.g., elements, factors, tests, etc.),

- Begins with an introduction or roadmap that outlines the analysis to follow

- Addresses each issue (or sub-issue or combined issues) in turn, moving from general rules to specific conclusions

- Uses headings where helpful to visually divide analysis

Small Scale: (p. 128)

- Paragraphs are a digestible length and limited to one or more related ideas (more than one page is usually difficult to follow)

- Topic sentences signal the subject of the paragraph in a meaningful way

- Sentence structure is not too complicated by stringing a series of clauses together

- States the general requirement or rule of law, including a synthesized rule where necessary to explain its meaning

- Explains the synthesized rule by discussing how courts have interpreted it (either in your text or explanatory parentheticals, p. 234)

- Uses analogical reasoning to analogize and distinguish case law where helpful, available, or necessary

- Analogies include adequate information about the facts, the holding, and an explicit comparison (as opposed to a simple description of the case that forces the reader to make the comparison herself)

- Discusses only reasonable counter-arguments and problematic law or cases.

- Each discussion of a discrete issue ends with a definitive conclusion that makes the writer's opinion clear

- Analysis uses more than one case per issue, where available and helpful to fully explain the law

Style

Is written in plain English (pp. 221–228)

The tone of the writing is objective (i.e., even-handed as opposed to argumentative)

Is concise (pp. 228–235)

Conforms to legal writing conventions (pp. 235–239)

Grammar and punctuation are correct (pp. 239–247)

Spelling and citations are correct

Conclusion

Summarizes the discussion in more detail than in the brief answer

Contains no citations to authority

4. LEGAL ADVICE VIA EMAIL

In today's fast-paced, global economy and with high-tech options readily available, lawyers often use email to communicate with other lawyers and clients. Of course email may contain legal advice just as legal memoranda do. But unlike legal memoranda, email does not have a universally recognized format derived from classical speech. As it has evolved, **legal email** tends to look like a stripped down legal memorandum designed for efficiency. If a legal memorandum is a luxury sedan—large, fully equipped, and expensive—then legal email is a hybrid—the product of new technology designed for the same purpose but compact and fuel efficient.

Unlike legal memoranda, the audience for email is never "the file." Email always represents part of a larger, ongoing conversation with a specific recipient in mind. For that reason, it is more immediate, more personal, and sometimes more stressful to write. It also carries a greater risk of being disclosed to the wrong people.

A. FORMAT OF LEGAL ADVICE VIA EMAIL

The format and tone of email advice depends on a number of factors, including whether the recipient is the client, another lawyer representing the same client, opposing counsel, or some other interested party. This section addresses the kind of email you might send to a supervising lawyer who asks you to "look into something" (i.e., conduct research on a specific legal issue and send her an email). Advice written directly to clients is addressed in more detail in Chapter 7.5. Email advice rarely looks exactly like a legal memorandum on a computer screen. Nor is it a summary of the analysis like a brief answer or conclusion in a legal memorandum.

To the extent there is a typical email format (legal email has evolved relatively recently), it usually begins with a **greeting**, followed by a **short introduction** that restates the legal issue the writer was asked to research, her overall findings or conclusions, and the most legally significant facts. There is rarely a separate section or paragraph that restates the facts; the relevant or key facts are usually known to the intended recipient.

The writer's **legal analysis** usually follows in a separate paragraph or paragraphs. Because email is more conversational, the analysis is often less formal and complete, in terms of laying out each component of a legal syllogism. You may find yourself assuming or combining parts of your analysis because your reader will not be confused. Depending on the complexity and number of issues, you may or may not need to begin with a detailed roadmap. If your reader already has enough context for the analysis to dispense with it, do so.

> **Legal email** often includes:
>
> - a greeting
> - a short introduction restating the issue, conclusion, and legally significant facts
> - detailed legal analysis with citations
> - a short conclusion that makes a recommendation or asks for next steps
> - closing
> - a confidentiality statement

As with all legal analysis, organize first by the issues (e.g., does the court have jurisdiction? What causes of action might the plaintiff pursue? What damages might be recoverable?). For each issue, organize based on the controlling rules of law relevant to each issue (e.g., the controlling test, elements, standard, factors, etc.). You may include headings, lists, and bullets to visually guide your reader, who will often be busy or rushed. Your small-scale organization should generally follow the analytical paradigm: issue→ rule→ application→ conclusion (p. 79). You should include citations, but depending on your office, you may not be expected to use a traditional format (when in doubt, use it). To the extent the email leaves out any portion of the analysis for the sake of expediency, be sure to specify what is being left out. The email should end with a **summary of your conclusion**, if necessary, or **any requested or recommended next steps**.

The tone of legal advice via email tends to be more casual and conversational than that of a memorandum. For example, although legal writers typically avoid using personal pronouns and contractions in formal legal writing, they are more likely to use them in email. People tend not to indent paragraphs either. Nevertheless, the email must still be professional: it should be well-written and proofed just as a memorandum would be.

The email should also contain a **confidentiality statement**. Because it can easily be forwarded to third parties, legal email presents a challenge in keeping client communications confidential and protecting the attorney-client privilege. As a practicing lawyer, you have an ethical obligation to keep your client's communications confidential. Anything your client discloses to you in confidence is also protected by the attorney-client privilege (a matter of state law). That means you cannot be required to testify about the content of those communications. However, if those communications are intentionally disclosed to third parties, they are no longer protected. If you accidentally send an email to a third party, you could put the privilege in jeopardy. Before sending or forwarding legal email, be sure to make sure that the recipient falls within the scope of the attorney-client privilege and would not be considered a third party.

Finally, email is an easy and quick way to deliver advice, *but it should not be sent in haste or anger.* Just like personal email, once you send it, you cannot get it back. Avoid sending email accidently. Leave the addressee section blank until the email message is complete and proofed. If you write an email while angry or frustrated, save it. Once you've calmed down and gained perspective, delete it. Find a better way to respond or not at all.

Below is an example of an email that a lawyer might send to her supervisor having been asked to conduct legal research on false disparagement in Texas for Starbucks.

B. SAMPLE EMAIL IN THE STARBUCKS MATTER

From: Sara Jan   Sent: Th 6/15/15 4:18 p.m.

To: jelkins@elkinsfirm.com

CC:

Subject: Starbucks/false disparagement

Attachments:

Jim:

You asked me to research the likelihood that Velas would succeed in a claim for false disparagement under the Texas statute. Assuming that the beans he sells "perish or decay in a limited period of time," he could probably establish a claim with respect to lost coffee bean sales. However, since coffee drinks are not products of agriculture, they likely do not qualify for protection. It would help to know the extent to which Starbucks' drop in sales can be attributed to beans as opposed to prepared drinks.

Short introduction that restates the issue researched and the writer's ultimate conclusion. It also raises a factual question as to the nature of the coffee beans and the extent to which Starbucks' sales losses are attributable to bean sales.

To succeed under the statute, Starbucks would have to prove the following three elements:

(1) that CSP disseminated the information to the public about a "perishable food product";

(2) that CSP knew its information was false; and

Legal analysis begins here with a short roadmap outlining the elements of a claim for false disparagement in Texas and the statutory remedy.

(3) that the newsletter stated or implied that the beans are unsafe for consumption.

Tex. Civ. Prac. & Rem. Code Ann. § 96.002 (a)–(c) (Vernon 2011). A person is liable to the producer of the perishable food product for damages and any other appropriate relief. § 96.002(b).[4]

Dissemination to the public.

Dissemination "to the public" means the information was distributed to a large enough audience to constitute the public in the ordinary sense of the word. *Green's Grocer v. Janus*, 228 S.W.2d 94, 95 (Tex. 2012). There, because the defendant made false statements during a local TV broadcast, it was disseminated to the public. *Id.* Although it is not certain, sending a newsletter to 50 subscribers is likely to qualify as the public, particularly since news of this sort tends to travel quickly.

A "perishable food product" (PFP) is "a food product of agriculture or aquaculture that is sold or distributed in a form that will perish or decay beyond marketability within a limited period of time." § 96.001. The product must be a sole food product, not a combination of products. *See The Pet Barn, Inc. v. Holmes*, 224 S.W.2d 99, 102 (Tex. 2004) (holding that a baked pet snack was not a product of agriculture even though it contained products of agriculture). Assuming coffee can be considered a food product, Starbucks beans are probably products of agriculture, but coffee drinks are not. Like baked pet snacks, most Starbucks coffee drinks are a combination of products of agriculture, such as sugar and milk. They also contain water. Extending protection to coffee drinks would be inconsistent with *Pet Barn* and impermissibly expand liability.

The headings quickly signal to the reader the organization of the analysis to follow.

Notice the more conversational tone but the same deductive form of reasoning with respect to each issue: rule→ application→ conclusion.

Separate paragraphs visually divide the analysis of the first element into its three sub-issues.

These first two sentences state the synthesized rule on perishable food products.

An explanatory parenthetical is used here in lieu of textual discussion to succinctly explain the rule from Pet Barn.

Application of rule to facts, including an analogy to Pet Barn.

Conclusion.

---

[4]   The extra spaces between paragraphs in the text of the email are to make room for the annotations at right.

Finally, the coffee beans must perish or decay within a limited period of time. § 96.001. Six months is likely too long to be considered a limited period of time, *id.* at 103, but since the "best before" date is six to eight weeks, and Starbucks cannot sell them past that date, we have a good argument that this portion of the element is satisfied. CSP could argue that coffee beans do not spoil like fresh produce or meat, but if the beans are no longer salable within six to eight weeks, they likely perish beyond marketability in a limited period of time.

Rule on perishable food product.

Application of rule.

Anticipation and resolution of counter-argument.

Knowledge of falsity.

Knowledge of falsity can include actual knowledge as well as a reckless indifference to truth. *Thomas Meats v. Safeway*, 10 S.W.3d 45 (Tex. 2007). There the defendant grocery store posted a sign in its windows saying that the plaintiff's meats were unsafe. Because the defendant failed to investigate the truth before posting the signs, the court held the store's "reckless indifference to the truth was tantamount to knowledge of falsity." *Id.* at 46. Given that CSP failed to investigate the nature of Starbucks' beans much as the store in *Thomas Meats* failed to investigate rumors about the meat it was selling, we should be able to prove CSP was recklessly indifferent to the truth.

Synthesized rule on knowledge of falsity.

The writer explains the rule from *Thomas Meats* in text because it would be difficult to capture in an explanatory parenthetical.

Conclusion.

Implies unsafe for public consumption.

To state or imply that a PFP is unsafe, the defendant must indicate that the product is inherently dangerous in some way. *Green's Grocer*, 228 S.W.2d at 95. In that case, the court held that a statement that a customer had choked on the plaintiff's apple did not qualify because it did not indicate there was anything wrong with the apple *per se*. *Id.* at 96. However, CSP implied that Starbucks' coffee beans are dangerous by associating them with pesticide use. Although CSP might argue it stated only that the beans are not organic as they are advertised, the fact that sales dropped precipitously appears to be evidence of their perceived danger.

Synthesized rule on what "states or implies" means.

Explanation of rule from *Green's Grocer*.

Application, including analogical reasoning to distinguish *Starbucks'* case.

Producer of a perishable food product.

Although several states limit "producer" to those who actually grow agricultural crops, *see, e.g.,* Fla. Stat. § 865.065 (2014) (limiting recovery to "the person who actually grows or produces" the food products), Texas does not. The legislative history also indicates that "unprocessed" was deleted from the definition of PFP "so the statute would apply to both processed and unprocessed food." H. Bill Analysis, 74–722, Reg. Sess., at 4 (Tex. 1995). Thus the fact that the beans are roasted does not appear to disqualify them from protection.

> Use of legislative history to interpret ambiguous term.

> Conclusion.

As I say, there is a good chance of Starbucks succeeding but only if coffee beans "perish or decay" in a limited period of time. When you meet with Velas, it would help to get a better idea of the reason and need for the "best before" dates and how much of his sales losses are attributable to bean sales.

> This paragraph reminds the reader of the writer's overall conclusion and the information still needed from the client. It also makes reference to a prior conversation, with which both reader and writer are familiar, about other ongoing work related to representing Starbucks.

Let me know if there is anything else you need from me before the meeting. I will continue research on the other options we discussed last week.

Sara

Sara Jan

The Elkins Firm

874 Main Street, Suite 130

Dallas, Texas 75034

214-993-9012

sjan@elkinsfirm.com

This email is confidential, protected by the attorney-client privilege, and intended only for the recipients listed above. If you receive it in error, please contact me at the above address and then destroy it.

> Confidentiality statement.

5. CLIENT OR OPINION LETTERS

When lawyers refer to **client letters** (also called **opinion letters**), they do not mean cover letters used to transmit documents or other information. This phrase is a term of art that usually refers to a letter formally stating the legal opinion (both research findings and conclusions) of a lawyer, law firm, governmental agency, or other organization with respect to work done on behalf of a client. For example, a cosmetics manufacturer might want advice on whether certain claims about its products comply with federal law. Before its legal department will approve proposed advertising for its new products, the manufacturer gets advice from an expert on food and drug law. So it retains outside counsel to provide that advice.

A. FORMAT OF A CLIENT LETTER

Client letters can be written for a variety of clients, including private individuals, government officials, lawyers, lawyers in private practice, and in-house counsel. They can advise clients on how to comply with administrative law, such as securities regulation, tax, education, immigration, or food and drug law. They can be written for other reasons as well, including how to structure a new business venture, how to respond to a criminal investigation, and whether to proceed with litigation or seek a different remedy. Any time a client wishes a formal opinion and the lawyer is willing to give one, it is likely to be in writing. Putting the opinion in writing protects both the lawyer and client by specifying the nature and scope of the opinion and the information on which it is based.

> A **client letter** should include:
>
> - a greeting
> - a short restatement of the issue and conclusion
> - the facts on which the opinion is based
> - any unknown facts
> - an explanation of the opinion with or without legal citations, depending on the client
> - a summary of the opinion
> - next steps
> - closing

Like legal advice via email, client letters have no universal format. The format used is likely to be specific to a particular area of practice or a particular law office. Because client letters make a law office vulnerable in the event the advice turns out to be "wrong," beginning lawyers are not often asked to write them. However, in the event you are asked to draft a client letter, first ask if there is a desired format or sample for you to use. In the absence of guidance, structure the letter loosely like a legal memorandum: state the **issue**, your **conclusion**, **the facts** on which the opinion is based, and any **unknown facts** that might alter the opinion.

Proceed to **explain your opinion** based on the law. This should resemble the discussion section of a memo in the sense that it is organized first by issue and then by the controlling rules of law. The tone and level of detail here will depend on the nature of the client. For example, if the client is a lawyer, you might write the letter in as much detail as you might the discussion section of a memorandum, including signals, citations to authority, and full explanations of your analysis. If the client is a layperson, you might need to spend more time explaining the law and use fewer citations to authority. If the client is not a lawyer but an executive of a large corporation used to reading legal analysis, you might do something in between. When in doubt, include citations to authority and let your supervisor take them out if necessary. At the end, **summarize** your opinion and make sure the client understands **what to do or expect next.**

Below is an example of a client letter that a senior lawyer might send to Velas, the owner of the Texas Starbucks, on the issue of whether to file suit against CSP under the Texas false disparagement statute. Given the difficulty establishing that roasted coffee beans perish or decay beyond marketability in a limited period of time, see pp. 85 and 125, the firm has chosen to recommend caution in filing suit as a first step. Notice that the writer includes some citations that preserve his thinking, communicate the support for the opinion, and add to the *ethos* of the opinion, but he has chosen not to overwhelm the client with too much detail. The writer also avoids using legal jargon, which can be both off-putting and confusing.

B. SAMPLE CLIENT LETTER IN THE STARBUCKS MATTER

The Elkins Firm

874 Main Street

Suite 130

Dallas, Texas 75034

214-993-9000

July 15, 2015

Ramon Velas

Starbucks Coffee Company

6223 Commerce St.

Suite #100

Dallas, TX 75034

Dear Mr. Velas:

I enjoyed meeting you last month and am pleased to advise you in this matter. In particular, you have asked for our opinion with respect to financial and other losses due to statements made by Citizens for Safe Products (CSP) about your coffee products. Having conducted the research we discussed and considered the facts as you described them, we believe at this time that your claim under the Texas false disparagement statute has merit but would likely fail. For that reason, we conclude it would be worthwhile to first attempt to negotiate with CSP to compensate you for at least some of your losses before considering filing suit.

> This paragraph restates the issue and the firm's overall conclusion.

This conclusion is based on the facts set forth below. If I have misunderstood or failed to include any facts you think significant, please let me know as soon as possible. Any change in these circumstances could change our opinion. CSP is a national non-profit corporation with a local chapter in Dallas. The chapter has roughly fifty members to whom it distributes its bi-monthly newsletter. The March newsletter was emailed to all members and claimed that the beans (ground and whole) and prepared coffee drinks you sell are not organic. To the best of your knowledge and belief, the beans are not grown using pesticides, as CSP claims, and are organic in all other respects. Also to the best of your knowledge, CSP made no effort to contact you, your suppliers, or Starbucks' headquarters about the nature of the beans. Since the newsletter was published, coffee bean and drink sales have dramatically declined, and customers have been asking questions related to the newsletter and the nature of the beans. You have also been required to remove bagged beans from your shelves because they were not sold by the "best before" date, which is roughly six to eight weeks after production. We would like to know more about the need for this pull date. Do the beans truly spoil or do they simply begin to lose flavor?

> The second paragraph states the facts on which the opinion is based and asks for clarification about an unknown fact.
>
> In a formal client letter, 50 is spelled out.

The Texas statute we discussed is designed primarily to protect Texas farmers. The law provides a remedy for false statements about the safety of their products because fruits, vegetables, meat, and fish often spoil before a farmer has a chance to reassure the public that the product is safe.

This paragraph begins the legal analysis and support for the conclusion. It starts by explaining the purpose behind the statute, which supports the ultimate conclusion that the claim here is not strong.

In order to succeed in a claim against CSP, we would have to prove three things we call "the elements" of a claim: First, we would need to establish that your products are food products of agriculture that "perish or decay beyond marketability within a limited period of time." Second, we would need to prove that CSP had knowledge that its statements were false, and third, that CSP stated or implied that your products are unsafe for consumption by the public. *See* Tex. Civ. Prac. & Rem. Code Ann. § 96.002 (a)–(c) (Vernon 2011).

This paragraph sets out a roadmap for the reader and explains what "elements" are because the client may be unfamiliar with that term.

As for the first element, coffee beans probably qualify as food products of agriculture. CSP might claim they are not food, since they carry little nutritional value, but they are grown, harvested, and ingested, in some form, like other agricultural crops, and they do contain minerals and antioxidants. The real issue is whether they "perish or decay" in a limited period of time. I understand that you do not sell your beans past the six to eight-week "best before" date, but a court might conclude that they do not spoil beyond marketability in the same way that heads of lettuce or cuts of meat do, and therefore, they are not intended to be protected under this statute. In addition, a court might also conclude that the statute protects only locally grown products, not those grown elsewhere and imported to Texas.

In this paragraph, the writer explains the law and the trouble they will have proving the first element.

Coffee drinks, on the other hand, are almost certainly not protected under the statute. First, there is a fairly recent Texas case indicating that the product must be a sole product of agriculture, not a combination of agricultural products. *The Pet Barn, Inc. v. Holmes*, 224 S.W.2d 99, 102 (Tex. 2004) (holding that a baked pet snack made of several agricultural products was not a

This paragraph explains that at best, only the beans are protected under the statute.

food product of agriculture). Since the coffee drinks you sell usually contain milk, sugar, and syrups, they are not sole products of agriculture. Second, these drinks cannot really be said to "perish or decay" because you do not prepare them ahead of time; you make them to order.

As for the second element, we could likely prove that CSP had knowledge that its statements were false. We cannot know what CSP members were thinking when they published the newsletter, but we do know they did not check with you or anyone else to verify their information. The Texas court has held that recklessness is equivalent to knowledge, *Thomas Meats v. Safeway,* 10 S.W.3d 45 (Tex. 2007), and CSP appears to have been reckless in failing to contact you, demonstrating "indifference to the truth" or falsity of its statements.

The writer continues to translate the law and explains in the next two paragraphs that they can likely prove the second and third elements as to lost bean sales.

As to the third element, we could likely prove that CSP implied that your products are unsafe for consumption by the public. As your lost sales demonstrate, people tend to think that chemicals make food "inherently dangerous in some way." *Green's Grocer v. Janus*, 228 S.W.2d 94, 95 (Tex. 2012). The Texas statute (and others like it) was enacted in response to a public scare in the late 1980s relating to the use of Alar, a chemical used to keep apples from falling off trees before they were ripe.

If these elements can be proved, the defendant is liable to the "producer of the perishable food product for damages and any other appropriate relief." § 96.002(b). The statute does not state that you must have grown the coffee beans, but CSP is likely to argue that it protects only Texas farmers, not those who resell food products purchased outside of Texas. The legislative history indicates that the statute is intended to include processed as well as unprocessed food products, which may help refute CSP's claim.

In sum, although we would likely be able to prove the second and third elements of the claim, we anticipate having difficulty proving that coffee

Here, the writer sums up the basis for the firm's ultimate conclusion.

beans are "food products of agriculture," that they "perish or decay beyond marketability within a limited period of time," and that you are a "producer" of the beans.

For these reasons, we recommend that we contact CSP prior to filing suit to notify them of our intent to file and discuss the possibility of their compensating you at least in part for your loss. As we discussed, I hope you have already posted signs in your store and published advertisements in the local paper explaining the confirmed organic nature of the beans. Please contact me at your earliest convenience to schedule a meeting to discuss a potential strategy for going forward.

> The writer recommends next steps and invites the client to schedule a meeting to discuss them.

Sincerely,

James U. Elkins

James U. Elkins, J.D.
214-993-9025
jelkins@elkinsfirm.com

---

6. BENCH MEMORANDA

Bench memoranda are written by law clerks to trial and appellate court judges to help them make decisions. In accordance with procedural rules, parties may make **motions** (requests to the judge to make a certain decision) before, during, or after trial. For example, if a defendant in a criminal case believes the evidence against her was obtained in violation of her rights, she could file a motion to exclude the evidence at trial. To help the judge rule on the motion, a law clerk might research the legal issues, evaluate the parties' arguments, and write her conclusions in the form of a bench memo.

At the appellate level, a law clerk reviews the entire record on appeal, conducts original research on the legal issues, evaluates the parties' arguments, and writes a bench memorandum to prepare the judge for oral argument. As a law student, you might write a bench memorandum in an upper-level writing course or as part of a moot court competition. If you decide to clerk for a state or federal court judge, you will most certainly write bench memos.

A. FORMAT OF A BENCH MEMORANDUM

There is no universal format for bench memoranda; each court or judge tends to have specific requirements. In general, they can be structured like legal memoranda with additional information helpful to the judge. In the absence of a prescribed format, use the following guidelines:[5] In the heading, include the caption of the case, the **docket number** (the number assigned to the case by a court clerk), the judge(s) involved, and the name of the lower court (if the case is now on appeal). The body of the memo should begin with a statement of the issues before the court. Depending on the judge, you may be required to state the issues as phrased by the moving party/appellant or from a more neutral point of view. Either here or after the discussion, state your **recommended ruling**. This is akin to your predicting the outcome on the issues in a legal memorandum.

A **bench memorandum** should include:

- The case caption, docket number, judge(s) involved, and the name of any lower court (if the case is now on appeal)

- a statement of the issues raised by the parties

- a recommended ruling (if requested)

- statement of the case, including the procedural history and current status

- a brief statement of the facts of the case

- standard of review (for appeals)

- discussion, including an overview of the law, a summary of the arguments raised by the parties, and your legal analysis (if requested)

- any matters to be addressed in court or during oral argument

Next give a **statement of the case** that includes the procedural history, the current status of the case, and if on appeal, the name of the lower court, the disposition below, and the party that filed the appeal. Your statement of the case should be followed by a brief and objective **statement of the facts.** In an appeal, you should not take the facts as stated by the parties for granted. You will need to verify the facts by checking them in the **record**. The record consists of all the documents and evidence that the appellate court receives from the lower court. Usually it is all collected and paginated as one document for easy reference. You will need to cite the record to support your statement of the facts. Also, it is easier for the judge if you refer to the parties by name. "Appellant" and "appellee" can be confusing.

---

[5] *See, e.g.,* FEDERAL JUDICIAL CENTER, LAW CLERK HANDBOOK: A HANDBOOK FOR LAW CLERKS TO FEDERAL JUDGES 90–95 (Sylvan A. Sobel, ed., 2d ed. 2007).

The **discussion** section follows and can include headings. For each issue, start with an **overview** of the law, akin to the roadmap in the discussion of a legal memorandum and proceed to explain the controlling rules of law. This familiarizes the judge with the law and puts the issues in context. Again, you cannot rely on the parties' statements of the law. They may be incomplete, inaccurate, or biased. The parties' arguments will provide a good starting point, but you need to verify that their characterizations of the law are accurate.

Proceed to summarize **each party's arguments** with respect to each issue. Your judge may want you to summarize only what the parties have actually argued. Some judges will also want you to give the parties' best arguments (i.e., the arguments they should have made).

At this point, if requested, give your **legal analysis** of the issues. You may state your recommended ruling here or directly after the statement of the issues. Finally, some judges will also want you to inform them of issues that the parties failed to address, matters that need to be clarified, or questions the judges might ask the parties.

Like client letters and legal memoranda, the tone of a bench memorandum is formal, and it should include proper citations to the record and legal authority. Unless your judge asks you to write as though you are the court speaking, you should write a bench memorandum from your own perspective.

Assume that Starbucks filed suit against CSP for false disparagement in a federal district court in Texas (see a sample complaint, pp. 175–179). (To review the facts of the Starbucks case, see Chapter 4.3, p. 61). CSP then filed a motion to dismiss for failure to state a claim under Fed. R. Civ. P. 12(b)(6), which the district court denied (see the sample motion and supporting memorandum on pp. 181 and 183–188). The case went to trial, and at the close of the plaintiff's case, CSP filed a motion for judgment as a matter of law under Federal Rule of Civil Procedure 50,[6] which the court granted. On the opposite page is a sample bench memorandum that might be written on appeal for the appellate judges prior to oral argument.

---

[6]   Fed R. Civ. P. 50(a)(1) states, "If a party has been fully heard on an issue during a jury trial and the court finds that a reasonable jury would not have a legally sufficient evidentiary basis to find for the party on that issue, the court may: (A) resolve the issue against the party; and (B) grant a motion for judgment as a matter of law against the party on a claim or defense that, under the controlling law, can be maintained or defeated only with a favorable finding on that issue.

B. SAMPLE BENCH MEMORANDUM IN THE STARBUCKS MATTER

To: Judges of the Fifth Court of Appeals of Texas

From: Law Clerk

Date: April 15, 2016

Re: *Starbucks v. CSP*, Docket No. 16–422CIV, on appeal from the Northern District of Texas, The Honorable S. White

Statement of the Issue

Whether the district court erred in granting Defendant's Motion for Judgment as a Matter of Law with respect to whether Starbucks is a producer of a perishable food product pursuant to Chapter 96 of the Texas Civil Practice and Remedies Code.

This is a relatively neutral statement of the issue. Starbucks might have stated it in any number of ways to be more persuasive. For ways to draft persuasive issue statements, see Chapter 9.4, p. 190.

Recommended Ruling

I recommend that Your Honors affirm the judgment of the United States District Court for the Northern District of Texas.

Statement of the Case

In September 2015, Ramon Velas, doing business as Starbucks, filed suit against Citizens for Safe Products (CSP) under the Texas false disparagement statute, Tex. Civ. Prac. & Rem. Code Ann. § 96.002 (Vernon 2011). It sought to recover losses allegedly due to statements CSP made in its March 2015 monthly newsletter. The case was filed in the United States District Court for the Northern District of Texas on September 21, 2015. At the close of the trial, the defendant moved for judgment as a matter of law, which the court granted on February 26, 2016. Judge White held that Starbucks is not a producer of a perishable food product: coffee is not a food product, coffee beans do not perish or decay "beyond marketability" in a limited period of time, and Starbucks resells the beans; it does not produce them. Thus, Starbucks is not entitled to protection under the statute." (R. at 1). Starbucks now appeals.

This is one typical citation format for citing the compiled record. Here, the citation is to page 1. Always check a court's local rules for their citing customs and requirements.

Statement of Facts

The appellant is the owner of a coffee shop, licensed and doing business as Starbucks, in Dallas, Texas. It attributes much of its success to its exclusive use of organically grown coffee beans from fair trade sources. (R. at 12). Starbucks imports its roasted beans primarily from Central and South America. None of the beans it uses or sells to make coffee beverages are grown in Texas. (R. at 13).[7]

Each of these facts is verified by checking and citing the record.

CSP is a Dallas-based consumer rights group that publishes a monthly newsletter about products sold in the Dallas area. In March 2015, CSP published its newsletter stating that Starbucks beans are grown using pesticides. (R. at 22). Starbucks put on uncontroverted evidence that CSP did not contact anyone to verify the information before it published the newsletter. (R. at 24).

Starbucks also put on evidence that almost immediately after the newsletter was distributed, Starbucks' coffee bean and beverage sales decreased significantly. Customers began to ask questions about the source of the beans. (R. at 16). This Starbucks location has disposed of hundreds of packages of whole and ground beans that did not sell by their "best before" dates, which range from six to eight weeks from the time of production. (R. at 18). These dates are set in consultation with bean suppliers. (R. at 19).

Standard of Review

This Court reviews the decision to grant judgment as a matter of law *de novo*, applying the same legal standard as the district court. *Texas Beef Grp. v. Winfrey*, 201 F.3d 680, 686 (5th Cir. 2000).

Standard of review is a term of art that refers to the level of deference the reviewing court must give to the lower court's decision. For more information on standard of review, see Chapter 9.5, p. 202.

---

[7]   The extra spaces between paragraphs in the text of the bench memorandum are to make room for the annotations at right.

Discussion

1. Overview of the law

Section 96.002 of the Texas false disparagement statute makes a person liable if

(a) the person disseminates in any manner information relating to a perishable food product to the public;

(b) the person knows the information is false; and

(c) the information states or implies that the perishable food product is not safe for consumption by the public.

Tex. Civ. Prac. & Rem. Code Ann. § 96.002 (a)−(c) (Vernon 2011). A perishable food product is defined as a "food product of agriculture or aquaculture that is sold or distributed in a form that will perish or decay beyond marketability within a limited period of time." § 96.001. A person liable under this statute is liable to the producer of the perishable food product for damages and any other appropriate relief arising from the person's dissemination of the information. § 96.002(b).

Several states like Texas passed these so-called "veggie libel" statutes in response to the Washington apple scare in the 1980s. The goal was to protect their local food economies. *See, e.g.,* Sara Lunsford Kohen, *What Ever Happened to Veggie Libel?: Why Plaintiffs Are Not Using Agricultural Product Disparagement Statutes*, 16 Drake J. Agric. L. 261, 267−68 (2011).

2. Parties' arguments

a. **Starbucks.** Starbucks argues that it is a producer of a perishable food product and its coffee beans are entitled to protection under the Texas false disparagement statute. The statute does not define "food product," but a perishable food product is defined as one that perishes or decays "beyond marketability" within a limited period of time. § 96.001.

> Here, the clerk provides an overview of the false disparagement statute, including its elements, the relevant definition, and the overall intent of the legislature.

> Since Starbucks is the appellant, its arguments are presented first.

As for coffee beans being food, Starbucks argues that "food" is generally understood to mean a nutritious substance ingested to maintain health and life. *See, e.g.,* OXFORD ENGLISH DICTIONARY 279 (7th ed. 2012). Even though we might not think of coffee as food, coffee beans do contain nutrients such as potassium and magnesium, as well as antioxidants, and thus qualify for protection under the statute. People also rely on the stimulant effect from the caffeine in coffee to "maintain health and life." Like wheat, coffee is ground and used to make a variety of food products.

Starbucks also argues that coffee beans perish or decay beyond marketability within a limited period of time. The statute does not define a limited period of time, but the Texas court has indicated in dicta that six months is not a limited period of time. *The Pet Barn, Inc. v. Holmes*, 224 S.W.2d 99, 103 (Tex. 2010). In contrast, the beans lose flavor and cannot be sold after their "best before" dates, about six to eight weeks after they are shipped. These dates are recommended by the bean suppliers, not Starbucks. Starbucks put on evidence that customers generally will not purchase bagged beans after their "best before" dates.

Finally, Starbucks argues that it is "the producer of a perishable food product." § 96.002(b). Unlike most states with false disparagement statutes, Texas does not restrict the meaning of "producer" to those who actually grow the products being sold. *See, e.g.,* Fla. Stat. § 865.065 (2014) (limiting recovery to "the person who actually grows or produces" the food products).

The legislative history also indicates that "unprocessed" was deleted from the definition of perishable food product so the bill would apply to both processed and unprocessed food. Since the meaning of "producer" is not limited either to growers or unprocessed food, the legislature intended to include a larger group of defendants, like Starbucks, who purchase and resell perishable food products in Texas. *See also Johnson v. GlobalSantaFe Offshore Servs.*, 799

F.3d 317, 325 (5th Cir. 2015 (holding that remedial legislation should be liberally construed).

b. CSP. CSP disputes that Starbucks is the producer of a perishable food product. First, CSP argues that coffee is not a food product. Food consists of protein, carbohydrate, and fat used by the body to sustain growth, repair, and vital processes and to furnish energy. *Merriam-Webster Dictionary* 324 (6th ed. 2014). Neither coffee beans nor brewed coffee meet this definition.

Although coffee beans may contain some minerals, they are not food in the ordinary sense of the word. *See United States v. Kaluza,* 780 F.3d 647, 658–59 (2015) (stating where the language of a statute is unambiguous, its terms should be given their plain and ordinary meaning). CSP also argues that calories convert into energy, and coffee has very few calories. Although the caffeine in coffee has a stimulant effect, it does not convert to energy in the sense that calories do.

CSP also argues that coffee beans do not "perish or decay" beyond marketability within a limited period of time. The statute protects producers of meat, fish, and produce, which spoil in days or weeks. *See* H. Bill Analysis, 74–722, Reg. Sess., at 1 (Tex. 1995). In *Pet Barn*, the court held that the product at issue was not a product of agriculture because it was a combination of agricultural products. 224 S.W.2d at 102. It went on to suggest that six months is too long to be "a limited period of time." *Id.* at 103. As *Pet Barn* indicates, several months do not constitute a "limited" period of time. One-and-a-half to two months here was more than adequate time for Starbucks to correct any false statements about its coffee. Finally, the beans do not spoil in the sense that they become inedible. As the "best before" phrase suggests, the beans simply lose flavor after that date.

Finally, CSP argues that Starbucks is not "the producer of a perishable food product." § 96.002(b). The false disparagement statute is intended to protect local farmers and the local economy. Starbucks is not a producer; it does not grow anything. It purchases beans from outside the United States and resells them. Even if it were considered a producer, the product it sells is not grown locally, and thus it is not protected by the statute.

3.   Analysis (if requested)

This Court should affirm the judgment granted below because CSP likely has the better argument. Even if coffee beans can be considered as food, they do not perish or decay beyond marketability in a limited period of time. Although the coffee beans lose flavor in six to eight weeks, they do not spoil. As CSP argues, the statute is intended to protect products such as fresh produce, meat, and fish, which spoil quickly, in a matter of days, before false statements can be corrected. Six to eight weeks seems to falls outside the legislature's concern. In addition, Starbucks cannot really be said to be a local producer as the statute contemplates. As CSP argues, it simply resells beans grown outside of Texas. It does not seem likely that the legislature intended to protect coffee bean producers outside of Texas. To extend liability here would include a host of plaintiffs the Texas legislature did not anticipate.

Here, the clerk gives the judges her opinion, which we would assume was requested by them. The clerk's memo, along with the parties' briefs, can serve as the basis for the appellate courts' written decision.

Questions for the Oral Argument

1. What did the Texas legislature intend to accomplish here? To protect Texas farmers or the Texas economy more generally?

2. Why is (or is not) coffee a food product?

3. Must the product be spoiled or inedible to perish or decay beyond marketability?

4. Why is (or is not) six to eight weeks a limited period of time?

5. Is "producer" an ambiguous term? Why?

6. Why should (or should not) "producer" include a merchant one step removed from the actual grower?

7. Must the food product be grown in Texas to qualify for protection? Why?

_____

CHAPTER 8

LEGAL ADVOCACY AND ARGUMENT

■ ■ ■

1. HOW DOES ADVOCACY DIFFER FROM ADVICE?

Legal advocacy differs from legal advice in in two major respects: **purpose** and **audience**. The purpose of legal advice is to inform and predict, whereas the purpose of legal advocacy is to argue and persuade. Here, appeals to logic, emotion, and credibility combine to convince the reader to make a decision in your client's favor. To change the status quo. The audience of a legal memorandum or email is usually restricted to the client and others who represent the client, so as not to jeopardize the attorney client privilege. In contrast, with rare exceptions, legal advocacy and legal argument take place in the presence of third parties or the public.

Legal advocacy is the heart and soul of all client representations. The nature of legal advocacy depends on the type of law you practice. A lawyer specializing in food and drug law might advise her clients how to comply with the law but then advocate against proposed changes to existing law. A transactional lawyer advocates for her client when negotiating a deal. And litigators[1] and trial lawyers advocate in anticipation or the midst of a lawsuit.

The next few sections in this chapter discuss *pathos* and *ethos* in legal advocacy. And, since many first year legal research and writing courses teach written legal advocacy through courtroom documents, the rest of the chapters discuss selected documents typically filed at the trial and appellate level in criminal and civil actions.

You will learn in Civil Procedure that most civil lawsuits begin with a **complaint**,[2] followed by an answer. Prior to and after trial, the parties may file **motions** that ask the court to do something: dismiss the complaint, exclude evidence, enter judgment in their favor, etc. These motions are supported by legal arguments set forth in **memoranda of points and authorities** (these sound predictive, but they aren't). A court's rules of criminal and civil procedure state when, how, and whether

---

[1] "Litigator" generally refers to a lawyer who represents large corporations or other entities in civil suits, where the bulk of the advocacy occurs prior to trial in "motions practice." Most litigators do not consider themselves trial lawyers.

[2] State and federal prosecutions begin with a complaint, information, or indictment.

> **Written legal advocacy** includes:
>
> - complaints
> - motions
> - memoranda of points and authorities
> - trial and appellate briefs

a party can file a particular motion. If a case goes to trial, the court may request a trial brief that sets out the facts still in dispute and the parties' legal arguments. On appeal, an **appellate brief** explains the issue on appeal and makes the party's arguments. Almost all documents like these that are filed with a court are generically referred to as briefs.

2. APPEALS TO *PATHOS* IN LEGAL ADVOCACY

A child accidentally breaks a vase and immediately blurts out, "I didn't mean it!" Her mother comes running to see what happened, and her daughter repeats, "I didn't mean it, Mom, I'm sorry." The child understands that since she broke the vase by accident, her mother's response is likely to be different from the one she would have had if her daughter broke the vase on purpose. The fact that it was an accident, combined with her daughter's apology, has an emotional impact that will affect the mother's response and any punishment the child receives.

As Aristotle put it, a speaker must get his audience "into the right state of mind."[3] In fact, he devoted more space in *Rhetoric* to emotional appeals than he did to logical appeals. Aristotle recognized that an audience is motivated to act only when it becomes emotionally involved and will make a decision in the speaker's favor only if the speaker has a sympathetic or better case. When we ask people why they decided to take a particular job, voted in a certain way, chose to marry, and so on, they invariably explain their feelings as well as their thought process. Reason and emotion are inextricably linked.

Regardless of the context, all legal advocates must make their audience favorably disposed to their arguments. In fact, Aristotle thought appeals to emotion were more critical in legal than other forms of argument. Referring to emotional appeals in criminal cases, he said, "To the friendly judge, the [defendant] will seem either quite innocent or guilty of no great wrong; to the inimical judge, the [defendant] will seem just the opposite."[4] He thought attorneys should be familiar with the range and complexity of human emotion so they can arouse the appropriate emotion in others.

According to Aristotle, there are three parts to emotional appeals: (1) the nature of the emotion itself, (2) the types of people and situations that make that emotion likely to occur, and (3) the causes of that emotion.[5] In

---

[3]   ARISTOTLE, RHETORIC, *supra* ch. 2 note 2, at bk. 2, ch. 1, p. 91.

[4]   ARISTOTLE, RHETORIC, *supra* ch. 2 note 2, at bk. 2, ch. 1, p. 91.

[5]   ARISTOTLE, RHETORIC, *supra* ch. 2 note 2, at bk. 2, ch. 1, p. 92.

Book 2 of *Rhetoric,* he examined the three components of anger, calm, love, hatred, fear, confidence, shame, benevolence, pity, indignation, envy, and emulation.[6] He defined anger as "an impulse, attended by pain, to a revenge that shall be evident, and caused by an obvious, unjustified slight with respect to the individual or his friends."[7] He observed that people become angry with those who insult or injure them in some way, and they are more likely to get angry with their friends than their enemies.[8] Aristotle advised lawyers to "represent the adversary as obnoxious in those things which make men angry, and as the sort of person who arouses anger."[9]

About emotional appeals, Quintilian said:

[T]he man who can carry the judge with him, and put him in whatever frame of mind he wishes, whose words move men to tears or anger, has always been a rare creature. Yet this is what dominates the courts, this is the eloquence that reigns supreme.[10]

The seventeenth century epistemologists also explored the idea that argument requires emotion to persuade. John Locke, for example, said that when a person is at ease, he is content without action. A person must be in a state of uneasiness, therefore, before he will act. To stir a person to uneasiness and action requires rhetoric—the arousal of emotion.[11] George Campbell, writing in the eighteenth century, also said that emotion is needed to stimulate action:

If the orator would prove successful, it is necessary that he engage in his service all these different powers of the mind, the imagination, the memory, and the passions. These are not the supplanters of reason, or even rivals in her sway; they are her handmaids, by whose ministry she is enabled to usher truth into the heart, and procure it there a favourable reception.[12]

This chapter discusses just a few ways to make effective emotional appeals and motivate your audience to take action in your client's favor. They include developing an overarching theory of the case, framing your client's story, and framing the law from your client's perspective. As you learn to craft emotional appeals, you may begin to feel uncomfortable, as though you are manipulating or "spinning" the facts. Any discomfort you feel in this regard can be traced back to Plato, who argued that rhetoric is

---

6   ARISTOTLE, RHETORIC, *supra* ch. 2 note 2, at bk. 2, ch. 1, pp. 93–131.

7   ARISTOTLE, RHETORIC, *supra* ch. 2 note 2, at bk. 2, ch. 2, p. 93.

8   ARISTOTLE, RHETORIC, *supra* ch. 2 note 2, at bk. 2, ch. 2, pp. 96–98.

9   ARISTOTLE, RHETORIC, *supra* ch. 2 note 2, at bk. 2, ch. 2, p. 99.

10   QUINTILIAN, INSTITUTES OF ORATORY, *supra* ch. 2 note 32, at bk. 6, ch. 2, p. 47.

11   LOCKE, *supra* ch. 6, note 4.

12   CAMPBELL, PHILOSOPHY OF RHETORIC, *supra* ch. 2 note 74, at 94.

a form of flattery and thus inferior to philosophy (see Chapter 2.2, pp. 19–21).

But lawyers have an ethical duty to advocate zealously for their clients.[13] Our judicial system is based on the expectation that both sides to a dispute will make their best arguments, and the judge or jury will decide the best truth under the circumstances. Just like the little girl who broke the vase, your client's best arguments appropriately include emotional appeals.

3. THEORY OF THE CASE

The theory of a case encapsulates the ultimate reason why the client should prevail in the course of any representation—in litigation, arbitration, negotiations, mediation, rule-making, etc. Having a theory of the case means being able to complete the following sentence: "My client should prevail because . . ." All arguments, both oral and written, that support the client's position should be consistent with the theory of the case. It incorporates appeals to reason and credibility, but the emphasis is usually on appeals to emotion.

In the Starbucks case, for example, Velas seeks damages caused by CSP's statements about the nature of the coffee beans he sells and uses to create coffee drinks. There is a Texas statute that protects producers of agricultural products, but Velas may have trouble convincing a court that in this context, he is a "producer" of an agricultural product that perishes or decays quickly enough to warrant protection, particularly since neither Velas nor Starbucks grows the beans. Why should Starbucks prevail in this matter? Is there anything about this particular Starbucks that makes recovery emotionally appealing here? What policy arguments support Starbucks' view?

> **Note:** The theory of the case captures the essence of the reasons why your client should prevail.

To craft a persuasive theory of the case, you would need to know more about your client. Assume that in meeting with Ramon Velas, you learned that he is indeed an independent licensee of the Starbucks brand (see Chapter 5.8, p. 110). He also grew up in Dallas, is married, and has twin eight-year-old boys. He owns just the one coffee shop in Dallas that opened in 2003. Since then, he has faced a number of setbacks. In 2012, he had to take out a second mortgage on his home to keep the business going. Apparently, he had a contract dispute with local bean suppliers who claimed he owed them monetary damages for improperly cancelling their contracts. To avoid an even more expensive lawsuit, he paid them.

---

[13] "A lawyer must also act with commitment and dedication to the interests of the client and with zeal in advocacy upon the client's behalf." MODEL RULES, *supra* ch. 6 note 8, at the Preamble.

More recently, he discovered that a CSP member owns one of the local bean supply companies Velas no longer uses. Velas has worked hard since the shop opened to use locally grown, organic ingredients. But coffee does not grow in Texas; it all has to be imported. He switched bean suppliers because he was not pleased with the beans' quality.

Do these facts change the way you think and feel about Velas' situation? How? It may help to visualize the mental image you'd want a judge, jury, or other decision maker to have of your client's situation once they have heard or read your argument. As the lawyer for Velas, you might want your audience to envision a small businessman being crushed under the weight of CSP. As a result, you might adopt the following theory: This small locally owned business, a licensee of Starbucks, should prevail because it provides a valuable product and community service that should not be jeopardized by the whims of uninformed and potentially dangerous consumer groups like CSP. What image does this evoke? Is it persuasive? What other theories can you think of? What might CSP's theory of the case be?

Clinton v. Jones, 520 U.S. 681 (1977), a real case, provides a great example of two effective but competing case theories. Paula Jones, a former Arkansas state employee, sued then-sitting President Clinton. She claimed that he had made sexual advances toward her while he was Governor of the State of Arkansas and that she was punished by her supervisors for rejecting him. Clinton claimed he was "immune from suit" while acting as President. Although the district court held that the trial could not go forward while Clinton was still in office, it held that discovery could proceed. 869 F. Supp. 690 (E.D. Ark. 1994).

Both parties appealed, and the United States Court of Appeals for the Eighth Circuit reversed. 72 F.3d 1354 (8th Cir. 1996). Clinton appealed to the United States Supreme Court. The parties' competing theories of the case are effectively woven throughout their written arguments. The Supreme Court ruled that President Clinton was not immune from suit for unofficial actions and that forcing him to defend himself while in office did not violate separation-of-powers principles. 520 U.S at 695, 703.

Clinton's and Jones' theories were in direct opposition. Clinton's goal was to postpone the trial. He argued he was too busy to take time away from the presidency to defend his case. He also argued that it would be an unconstitutional violation of the separation of powers for the judiciary to tell the Chief Executive what to do. In sum, his theory was that he was immune from suit because the Presidency is a special office, and presidents should not be bothered with defending against civil suits while in office.[14]

---

[14]   *See* Brief of Petitioner, *Clinton v. Jones*, No. 95–1853, 520 U.S. 681 (1997).

Jones, on the other hand, said the President should not be permitted to use his official position to avoid trial when sued as a private citizen for sexual harassment. She argued that as a practical matter, Clinton would have no trouble carrying out the duties of his office and defending himself at the same time. In sum, her theory was that the trial should go forward because the president is a man like any other man. Requiring him to answer for his actions did not interfere with his presidential duties in any way.[15]

What images do these theories evoke? Which one do you find more convincing? Why?

4. FRAMING YOUR CLIENT'S STORY

At every opportunity, advocates characterize their client's situation from their client's perspective. The goal is to make the audience (e.g., an opposing party or decision maker) sympathize with the client and want to respond favorably. The key is to take your client's situation and turn it into a compelling story, one that fits with your theory of the case. But how do you develop a compelling story?

Generally speaking, a story is a series of events involving a central character and secondary characters. The central character usually faces some sort of conflict or dilemma that ultimately gets resolved. A good story can be understood in terms of its essential elements: character, conflict, resolution, and plot (see chapter 5.8).

Character. Think of your client (not you) as the central character of the story. How can you best characterize your client? As an individual? An accused? Society? A corporation? An agency? The central character of your client's story could even be an inanimate object or an idea, like a piece of valuable property that both parties want to control.[16]

> To **frame your client's story,** consider
>
> - how to cast your client as "hero"
> - what role the other parties play
> - the nature of the client's conflict
> - how to resolve the conflict
> - the storyline or plot

In the Starbucks case, we might characterize the client in a number of ways: "just one man," "a regular guy," "the victim of defamation," "a small businessman," "a successful entrepreneur," "part of a multi-billion dollar corporation," etc. There is no right answer in the face of countless options, but "small businessman" seems like a good choice. It's consistent with the theory of the case (i.e., Starbucks provides a valuable

---

[15] *See* Brief of Respondent, *Clinton v. Jones,* No. 95–1853, 520 U.S. 681 (1997).

[16] *See* Stephen Paskey, *The Law is Made of Stories Erasing the False Dichotomy Between Stories and Legal Rules,* 11 LEGAL COMM. & RHETORIC: J. ALWD 51, 66 (2014).

product and community service that should not be jeopardized by the whims of uninformed and potentially dangerous consumer groups like CSP), and it humanizes the face of Starbucks without seeming melodramatic.

Certain stories are embedded deep in our psyche and resonate with all people (e.g., two people meet, fall in love, get married). These familiar or "stock stories" often feature familiar central characters or hero types. The mythologist Joseph Campbell believed that all cultures develop stories about certain hero types: the warrior, creator, caregiver, everyman, and explorer.[17] As Professor Ruth Anne Robbins explains, these hero types are based on the work of psychologists, such as Carl Jung, and anthropologists, such as Andrew Bastian.[18]

Robbins and other experts on storytelling recommend that lawyers consider whether these stock stories and hero types provide a good starting point for framing a client's story.[19] Although people play many roles in life (e.g., student, teacher, parent, child, friend, etc.), one of those may help you frame a compelling story in the context of your client's legal goals. Being a hero does not mean your client cannot have flaws.[20] Flaws help us relate to the hero and his plight. Although it may be tempting, avoid casting your client's opponent as the villain of the story (you don't really need one). The opponent may then counter by casting your client in that role, which is almost always impossible to defend. You also run the risk of overstating your case and damaging your credibility. Better to treat the opponent as some sort of obstacle to be overcome.[21]

Given what you now know about Ramon Velas, what hero type does he resemble most? Warrior? Creator? Caregiver? Everyman? Explorer? Given Velas' struggle to keep his business going and his efforts to use locally grown, organic ingredients to serve a unique, quality product, he could easily be a creator or an everyman. Since the goal of the Texas statute is to protect the local economy, and CSP has interfered with Velas' ability to deliver a unique product, "creator" may be the better choice, but again, there is no right answer.

Conflict and resolution. Conflict is what makes a story interesting, suspenseful, and exciting. There are universally recognized types of conflicts too. They include person v. person, person v. self, person

---

[17]   *See, e.g.,* JOSEPH CAMPBELL, THE HERO WITH A THOUSAND FACES, chs. III–IV (Comm. ed. 2004).

[18]   *See* Robbins, *Harry Potter, Ruby Slippers, and Merlin, supra* ch. 5 note 30, at 773; 7 THE COLLECTED WORKS OF C. G. JUNG, ch. VII (Sir Herbert Read, Michael Fordham, & Gerhard Adler, eds. 1966).

[19]   *See, e.g.,* RUTH ANNE ROBBINS, STEVE JOHANSEN, & KEN CHESTEK, YOUR CLIENT'S STORY: PERSUASIVE LEGAL WRITING 89–90 (2013); Robbins, *Harry Potter, Ruby Slippers, and Merlin, supra* ch. 5 note 30, at 802, App. I. The full list of hero types includes the outlaw/destroyer, scholar/sage, magician, ruler, lover, jester/fool, and innocent.

[20]   ROBBINS, JOHANSEN, & CHESTEK, YOUR CLIENT'S STORY, *supra* note 19, at 92.

[21]   *See* Robbins, *Harry Potter, Ruby Slippers, and Merlin, supra* ch. 5 note 30, at 786–88.

v. nature, person v. society, and person v. machine.[22] Just as stock stories and hero types may help you define your client's role in his or her own story, the nature of the conflict may help you frame that story. The conflict that gives rise to the dispute should bring out, not conflict with, your client's character. Although the nature of the conflict is important, your client's response to the conflict is more important. That's what the audience will care about.[23]

What is the nature of Ramon Velas' conflict? Person v. person? Person v. machine? CSP seems to have attacked Velas without verifying its information but for no apparent reason. Is it because one of Starbucks' former bean suppliers is owned by a member of CSP? If so, this dispute could really be about the former supplier versus Velas (i.e., person v. person). But we cannot assume CSP claimed the beans are not organic for that reason. The better choice might be to think of the conflict as person v. machine, where CSP is "the machine" working to protect consumers by safeguarding our food supply but without regard to the damage it causes the small businessman. Here, the machine's power is crushing Velas' business.

If you cast your client as a sympathetic figure in the midst of a troubling conflict, the audience will want to **resolve** the conflict with a happy ending (i.e., work toward or decide in your favor). To do that, you must propose a resolution that is consistent with the story you tell.[24]

Plot. Finally, your client's story needs a plot. The plot is the series of events that give rise to the conflict. Where does it start? Which details matter? How should it end? Fiction writers describe a good plot as containing the following stages: an introduction, a complicating incident or rising action, a climax, a resolution or falling action, and a denouement.[25] Stories usually begin calmly. The characters and setting are introduced, and then a conflict arises. The climax is the point at which it all comes together and the reader is anxious to know how the story will end. The resolution answers the question of how the story will end. The denouement is the conclusion of the story.

In the Starbucks case, you would need to decide first where the story starts. When Velas opened the shop? When he had to take out a second mortgage to keep the business going? With the publication of the CSP newsletter? If the story should start in a state of relative calm, perhaps it begins with Velas having finally found quality organic beans that his customers like and have come to value **(introduction)**. Then, out of the blue (or not), a consumer safety group publishes a newsletter claiming

---

[22] *See, e.g.,* Kenneth D. Chestek, *The Plot Thickens: The Appellate Brief as Story,* 14 J. LEG. WRITING 127, 140–41 (2008); Foley & Robbins, *Fiction 101, supra* ch. 5 note 29, at 469.

[23] Foley & Robbins, *Fiction 101, supra* ch. 5 note 29, at 469.

[24] Foley & Robbins, *Fiction 101, supra* ch. 5 note 29, at 472.

[25] Chestek, *supra* note 22, at 147.

that the beans are not organic as Velas has advertised. His customers start asking questions and stop buying his products **(complicating incident or rising action)**. As the "best before" dates come and go, Velas must pull coffee beans from the shelves. Soon thereafter, his business is once again in trouble **(approaching the climax)**. How will the story end? That's the question you want your reader to ask, but you cannot know the answer to that question until the dispute is resolved.

How else might you tell the same story? Put yourself in the role of lawyer for CSP. How would you cast CSP here? What kind of hero is CSP? What is the nature of CSP's conflict? And what series of events would CSP select to write the plot?

ADDITIONAL INFORMATION

WILLIAM GOLDMAN, ADVENTURES IN THE SCREEN TRADE: A PERSONAL VIEW OF HOLLYWOOD AND SCREENWRITING (1983).

JACK HART, STORY CRAFT: THE COMPLETE GUIDE TO WRITING NARRATIVE NONFICTION (2011).

PHILIP N. MEYER, STORYTELLING FOR LAWYERS (2014).

---

5. FRAMING THE LAW FROM YOUR CLIENT'S PERSPECTIVE

Emotional appeals do not occur just in the framing of the facts. They are used to frame the law as well. Rules of law and the policies behind them can always be characterized from your client's perspective. For example, the Fourth Amendment to the United States Constitution prohibits unreasonable searches and seizures.[26] From a criminal defendant's perspective, the Fourth Amendment *prohibits* police from searching his home unless they have a warrant issued by a judge based on probable cause that specifies with particularity the items to be seized. But from the prosecution's perspective, the Fourth Amendment *entitles* the police to search a home as long as they have probable cause to believe a crime has been committed, the items they seek are likely to be in the home, and a judge has issued a proper warrant.

It takes practice seeing the law from both sides, so don't be discouraged at first. You will need to have conducted thorough research and gained a full understanding of the law to do it well. Knowing how to frame the law from your client's perspective will help you tell your client's

---

[26] "The right of the people to be secure in their persons, houses, papers, and effects, against unreasonable searches and seizures, shall not be violated, and no Warrants shall issue, but upon probable cause, supported by Oath or affirmation, and particularly describing the place to be searched, and the persons or things to be seized." U.S. Const. amend. IV.

story, select the best cases to rely on in support of your legal rules, and make favorable analogies. Although you cannot distort or misrepresent rules of law,[27] you can state them in such a way as to favor your client's position.

How might you frame the overall goals of the Texas false disparagement statute from Starbucks' perspective? Recall that the Texas statute does not explicitly limit "producers" to those who actually grow the perishable products. From Starbucks' perspective then, the false disparagement statute might prohibit a person from making false statements about the safety of a perishable food product of agriculture or aquaculture and holds that person liable to the seller of that product. How would CSP characterize the law?

The specific requirements or rules of law can also be framed from Starbucks' perspective. Review the sample legal memorandum from Chapter 7.1, pp. 121–127. A legal memorandum often serves as a starting point for litigation. To give you an idea of how to rewrite legal rules from your client's perspective, read the chart below. Each synthesized rule of law is rewritten from Starbucks' perspective. This is where the art of advocacy truly comes into play. There are always many options. This is just one example. Each reframed rule sets up the argument to follow.

Element of the Texas statute	Neutral rule	Rule from Starbucks' perspective
First dissemination to the public	The audience must be large enough to constitute the "public" in the ordinary sense of the word. *Green's Grocer v. Janus*, 228 S.W.2d 94, 95 (Tex. 2012).	Information is disseminated to the public as long as there are enough people who receive it to constitute the "public" in the ordinary sense of the word. *Green's Grocer v. Janus*, 228 S.W.2d 94, 95 (Tex. 2012).
food product	"Food" is generally understood to mean a nutritious substance ingested to maintain health and life. *See, e.g.*, OXFORD ENGLISH DICTIONARY 279 (7th ed. 2012).	Any nutritious substance ingested to maintain health and life constitutes a food product. *See, e.g.*, OXFORD ENGLISH DICTIONARY 279 (7th ed. 2012).

---

[27] Lawyers have an ethical obligation to state the law accurately. MODEL RULES, *supra* ch. 6 note 8, at r. 3.3.

perishable food product	The statute does not define "limited period of time," but since it is designed to protect sellers of meat, fish, and produce, it likely refers to days or weeks as opposed to several months.	A food product perishes or decays in a limited period of time if, within several weeks or even a few months, it spoils, rots, or diminishes in quality such that it can no longer be sold to the public. *See* OXFORD DICTIONARIES, *http://www.oxforddictionaries.com/definition/english/limited* (defining "limited" as restricted in size, amount, or extent).
producer	Unlike other states, Texas does not limit the definition of producer to those who actually grow the crops. *See, e.g.,* Fla. Stat. § 865.065 (2014) (limiting recovery to "the person who actually grows or produces" the food products).	The producer of a perishable food product is any person who sells a perishable food product of agriculture or aquaculture. *Compare* § 96.001 *with* Fla. Stat. § 865.065 (2014) (limiting recovery to "the person who actually grows or produces" the food products).
Second	Knowledge of falsity can include actual knowledge as well as a reckless indifference to truth. *Thomas Meats v. Safeway,* 10 S.W.3d 45 (Tex. 2007).	Where the defendant acts with reckless indifference to the truth, it acts with knowledge of falsity. *Thomas Meats v. Safeway,* 10 S.W.3d 45 (Tex. 2007).
Third	To state or imply that a perishable food product is unsafe, the defendant must indicate that the product is inherently dangerous in some way. *Green's Grocer,* 228 S.W.2d at 95.	If the false statements imply that the perishable food product is inherently dangerous in some way, they imply the food product is unsafe. *Green's Grocer,* 228 S.W.2d at 95.

Using the same neutral rules of law, try to frame them from CSP's perspective. Which rules seem more convincing?

6. APPEALS TO *ETHOS* IN LEGAL ADVOCACY

Ethical appeals are even more important in legal advocacy than legal advice. Aristotle said a speaker must have a good character and be credible: "He must give the right impression of himself, and get his judge into the right state of mind."[28] Cicero said a speaker must make his audience "well-disposed, attentive, and receptive."[29] Quintilian developed an even broader view of ethos than Aristotle or Cicero: *ethos* encompasses more than the speaker's appeal at the time a speech is delivered; "a good man skilled in speaking" is a person free from vice, a lover of wisdom, a sincere believer in his cause, and a servant of the people.[30]

Michael Smith, a professor at University of Wyoming School of Law, describes *ethos* in legal writing as intelligence, character, and good will.[31] Intelligence is demonstrated by being well-informed, competent, empathetic, articulate, and creative.[32] Character is demonstrated by truthfulness, candor, zeal and professionalism.[33] Good will is the extent to which the reader respects the writer's motivation.[34]

Ethos in legal writing requires   • a good character, and   • credibility

The need to demonstrate good character can involve conflicting goals and duties. On the one hand, lawyers have an ethical duty to "zealously assert[ ] the client's position under the rules of the adversary system."[35] On the other hand, lawyers also act as officers of the court and must be candid with the tribunal (a court or other decision-making body). Under the Model Rules of Professional Conduct, lawyers cannot make false statements "of fact or law," must disclose "legal authority in the controlling jurisdiction known to the lawyer to be directly adverse to the position of the client and not disclosed by opposing counsel," and "cannot offer evidence the lawyer knows to be false."[36]

At what point do these duties intersect? At what point does fulfilling the duty of zealous advocacy conflict with the duty of candor to the tribunal? How far can you go in telling your client's story without beginning to mislead the court? How far can you go in framing rules of

---

[28]   ARISTOTLE, RHETORIC, *supra* ch. 2 note 2, at bk. 2, ch. 1, p. 91.

[29]   2 CICERO, DE INVENTIONE, *supra* ch. 2 note 26, at ch. 15, ¶ 20, p. 41.

[30]   QUINTILIAN, INSTITUTIO ORATORIO, *supra* ch. 2 note 32, at bk. 12, ch. 1, pp. 197–203.

[31]   MICHAEL R. SMITH, ADVANCED LEGAL WRITING: THEORIES AND STRATEGIES IN PERSUASIVE WRITING 127 (3d ed. 2013).

[32]   *Id.* at 149–89.

[33]   *Id.* at 127–44.

[34]   *Id.* at 144–47.

[35]   MODEL RULES, *supra* ch. 6 note 8, at the Preamble.

[36]   MODEL RULES, *supra* ch. 6 note 8, at r. 3.3(a)(1)–(3).

full-fledged attorneys. And the argument founders completely in the tide of state statutes and court rules authorizing law students, under appropriate circumstances, to undertake functions of licensed attorneys, including actual representation of clients before a court. . . . [W]e cannot condone a concept of attorneys' fees so narrow as to exclude the work of law students simply because they are not yet members of the bar.[10]

The Department of Employment Services does not take issue with these principles; it acknowledges that an application for an award of reasonable attorney's fees under § 1–623.27(b)(2) properly may seek compensation for the work of non-attorneys, including law students, who assisted an attorney in the successful prosecution of a claim. The Department disputes only that the law students rendered that type of assistance here. They did not do so, the Department argues, because as the CRB stated, "the two students directly represented [Ms. Copeland] in court and engaged in the limited practice of law" themselves.

[3] [4] This analysis is faulty. The fact that, as in *Jordan,* the law students permissibly "perform[ed] tasks that otherwise would [have] fall[en] to full-fledged attorneys" is not enough to exclude their work from the purview of the attorney's fee statute. The critical point is that Ms. ***336** Copeland was not represented before the Department by the law students alone; she was represented by the law students together with Professor Gutman, a licensed attorney-at-law under whose direction the students did their work. This was in accordance with the Rules of this Court. Rule 48 permits eligible law students to engage in "the limited practice of law" and appear before the District's courts and administrative tribunals on behalf of indigent clients, provided they do so as part of a law school clinical program and work under the direction of a "supervising lawyer."[11] The "supervising lawyer" must be an "active" member of the District of Columbia Bar;[12] must "[a]ssume full responsibility for guiding the student's work . . . and for supervising the quality" of that work;[13] must do everything "necessary in [his or her] professional judgment to insure that the student's participation is effective on behalf of the indigent person represented";[14] and must sign all pleadings and other documents to be filed in

---

10   *Id.,* 223 U.S. App. D.C. at 332–33, 691 F.2d at 522–23.

11   D.C. App. R. 48(a)(1).

12   *Id.,* R. 48(e)(4).

13   *Id.,* R. 48(e)(2).

14   *Id.,* R. 48(e)(3).

the matter.[15] Under the Rules of Professional Conduct, a lawyer having such "direct supervisory authority" over a non-lawyer in the practice of law is obliged to make "reasonable efforts to ensure" that the non-lawyer's conduct is "compatible with" the lawyer's own professional obligations and may be held "responsible for conduct of such a person that would be a violation of the Rules ... if engaged in by a lawyer."[16] Given these requirements, the "supervising lawyer" clearly has an attorney-client relationship with the law students' client and is personally responsible for her representation.

In this case, the "supervising lawyer" was Professor Gutman. The detailed time records submitted in support of the fee application confirm his assiduous supervision of the law students who handled Ms. Copeland's case.[17] As the administrative law judge recognized in the order reinstating Ms. Copeland's disability benefits, Professor Gutman was her legal counsel.

[5] Thus, contrary to the Department's characterization, this was not a case of lay representation before the Department. Ms. Copeland "utilized the services of an attorney-at-law in the successful prosecution" of her claim, and the law students who assisted her pursuant to Rule 48 did so under that attorney's direction and control. The CRB therefore erred as a matter of law in concluding that the students' work was not compensable in a reasonable attorney's fee award under D.C. Code § 1–623.27(b)(2).

> Holding

Accordingly, we reverse the decision of the CRB and remand this case for an administrative law judge to consider the fee application on its merits and award a reasonable attorney's fee.[18]

> Disposition

---

[15] *Id.*, R. 48(d)(1)(i).

[16] D.C. Rules of Prof'l Conduct R. 5.3(b), (c).

[17] According to the time records, Professor Gutman devoted considerable time providing his students with guidance and reviewing and correcting their work product. In preparing for Ms. Copeland's hearing, the students had weekly meetings with Gutman to discuss the case. Among other things, Gutman helped them with discovery and pleadings; advised them with respect to legal issues; and prepared them to conduct the hearing.

[18] We note that the fee application asks for payment to be made to the George Washington University Legal Clinics ("GWULC"), not to Professor Gutman. The Department has not argued that payment directly to GWULC at Professor Gutman's request would be impermissible in light of the requirement in D.C. Code § 1–623.27(b)(2) that the attorney's fee award be paid directly to the attorney, nor do we suppose it would be. *See Jordan*, 223 U.S. App. D.C. at 328 n. 14, 691 F.2d at 517 n. 14.

APPENDIX B

SAMPLE CASE BRIEFS OF *COPELAND V. DISTRICT OF COLUMBIA DEPARTMENT OF EMPLOYMENT SERVICES*[1]

■ ■ ■

SAMPLE 1

Facts
- D.C. government employee Copeland (C) sustained back injury at work and got benefits
- Department of Employment Services terminated benefits—condition held not related to work injury
- C filed request for administrative hearing
- C represented by two GW law students at Justice Advocacy Clinic under supervision of professor Gutman (G), a member of the D.C. bar
- Hearing judge reinstated benefits
- G and students filed for attorney's fees under D.C. Code § 1–623.27(b)(2) (only half their time)

Procedural History
- 9/8/08 chief hearing judge denied fee application since students not attorneys
- C filed appeal of decision denying fees

Issue

Does D.C. Code 1–623.27(b)(2) prevent an award of attorney's fees where the claimant was represented by law students participating in a clinical program under a lawyer's supervision?

Holding   No

Reasoning
- D.C. code permits recovery of fees for work "performed in support of, pursuant to, and under the direction of, an attorney-at-law"
- D.C.'s distinction between non-attorneys working "in support of, pursuant to, and under the direction of" attorneys and non-attorneys who directly represent claimants is untenable
- 623.27(b)(2) is patterned on D.C.'s Workers Compensation Act which has been held to include paralegal work; presumption is that when legislature imports language with settled meaning it intends for it to be interpreted in same way
- 42 U.S.C. § 1988 interpreted to mean more than actual members of the bar
- *Jordan v. United States Department of Justice* involved clinic students under federal law
- Students here acted under G's direction just as paraprofessionals do

Result   Reversed and remanded to award appropriate fee

---

[1]   3 A.2d 331 (D.C. 2010).

SAMPLE 2

Facts:

— DC employee prevailed in compensation-related suit rep'd by law students in clinic supervised by licensed atty prof

— Students/prof applied for atty's fees (1/2 time only, no time for prof)

— ALJ recognized prof as 'legal counsel'

Procedural History:

— ALJ denied award of atty's fees where plaintiff was represented by law students (supervised by atty.); CRB affirmed

Legal Issue(s):

— Whether work done by supervised law students in representing plaintiff amounted to representation by an attorney or a layperson (under CMPA)

Holding:

— CRB erred in concluding law students' work not compensable re atty's fees award under Comp Merit Personnel Act

Reasoning:

— Law student work parallels paralegal work (in that it contributes to work product of supervising atty)

— Law student work parallels 'full-fledged' atty work (in that law students do work that would otherwise fall to full attys during summer assoc/part-time jobs, as long as 'limited practice of law')

— BUT law students DO NOT = lay representation because of teaching, supervision, and review of licensed atty (creating atty-client relationship between prof/plaintiff)

— To exclude law student work would be anomaly among fee-shifting statutes

Result:

— Reversed and remanded for ALJ to consider on merits and award reasonable atty's fees

APPENDIX C

SAMPLE LEGAL MEMORANDUM

■ ■ ■

Legal Memorandum

To: Kim Janney

From: Ben Golum

Date: February 12, 2016

Re: Knox/WPA Claim

Question Presented

Under the Michigan Whistleblowers' Protection Act (WPA), did Good Hope Hospital commit retaliatory discharge when it fired Kathy Knox after she threatened to report the director of the hospital's blood bank to the FDA for distributing allegedly tainted blood?

Controlling law

Legal question

Legally significant facts

Brief Answer

Probably. The WPA requires that the plaintiff prove three elements, only two of which are at issue: (1) that she was engaged in protected activity, (2) discharged, and (3) there is a causal connection between her threat to report to a public body and her discharge. Neither party disputes that Knox has been discharged or that the FDA is a public body.

The Brief Answer begins with a short phrase that telegraphs the ultimate prediction.

The writer quickly explains what the elements of the claim are and which need analysis.

With respect to the first element, Knox is likely to establish that she was engaged in "protected activity" under the WPA because she was "about to" report a suspected violation to the FDA. She will also likely establish that she was about to report a "suspected violation" because even though she cannot point to a specific rule violation, she was acting in good faith and reasonably believed that using blood stored at improper temperatures violated

The second and third sentences explain the writer's prediction as to the first element and her reasoning.

federal regulations. With respect to the third element, Knox can likely establish a causal connection between her threat to report and her discharge. She was fired within a week of threatening to report; both the director of the blood bank and Knox's supervisor, Kleusing, were upset that she wanted to report; and Knox had an excellent performance record. For these reasons, any legitimate reason the defendant gave for firing Knox is likely a pretext.

This and the previous sentence explain the writer's prediction as to the third element and her reasoning.

The writer states here her overall conclusion.

Statement of Facts

Kathy Knox is a registered nurse who began working at Good Hope Hospital ("the hospital") in 2010. She was responsible for retrieving blood from and returning unused blood to the hospital's blood bank. Knox routinely kept track of the blood units she received, and placed the blood in the refrigerator for surgical use.

Comma not needed (after "received") with a compound verb. Ch. 10.5F

In the summer of 2015, Knox began to notice that the refrigerator was registering a higher temperature than FDA regulations permit. Knox asked the hospital maintenance department to examine the refrigerator and a few days later, they told her it was working properly. However, she still felt certain it was warmer than usual. On June 15, Knox told Mimi Betz, the director of the blood bank, about the potential problem with the refrigerator and suggested that she discard the blood that had been stored in it. The next day, when Knox returned unused blood to the blood bank, Betz told her the maintenance department said the refrigerator was fine, and Knox should focus on her own job.

Strive to be concise: just say "noticed." Ch. 10.3H

A comma is needed before "and a few days later" because "and" acts as a coordinating conjunction. Ch. 10.5F

The word "she" here is ambiguous; it's better to say "Betz." Ch. 10.5N

On June 20, Knox noticed that one of the blood units she suspected was tainted had been given back to her. When she questioned the safety of that particular unit of blood, Betz told Knox she was getting tired of Knox's complaints and that she would not "toss perfectly good product" just because Knox imagined there was some problem with it. Knox said something like: "I care about my patient's safety. If you give me any more bad blood, I am going to the FDA". Within minutes, Betz told Jon Kleusing,

Improper quotation placement; it should be: ". . . FDA." Ch. 10.5A

Knox's supervisor, about Knox's threat. Kleusing fired Knox one week later, claiming he had received complaints from co-workers that she was difficult to work with. When Knox asked Kleusing whether firing her was due to her interaction with Betz, Kleusing did not respond but reminded Knox that she had been reprimanded once in 2014 for complaints from a patient's parents. According to Knox, all the nurses who cared for that patient received complaints, but none of them was reprimanded or terminated.

Ms. Knox would like to know if she can successfully sue her employer for retaliatory discharge under the Michigan Whistleblowers' Act.

Discussion

Courts analyze claims filed under the WPA using a burden-shifting framework similar to that used in employment-related claims filed under the federal and state Civil Rights Acts. *Cooney v. Bob Evans Farm*, 645 F. Supp. 2d 620, 628 (E.D. Mich. 2009); *Taylor v. Modern Engineering, Inc.*, 653 N.W.2d 625, 630 (2002). If the plaintiff can make a prima facie claim of retaliatory discharge, the burden shifts to the defendant to articulate a legitimate reason for the discharge. *Roulston v. Tendercare, Inc.*, 608 N.W.2d 525, 530 (2000). If the defendant can establish a legitimate reason, the plaintiff may establish that the reason offered by the defendant is a pretext. *Id.*

To state a prima facie claim under the WPA, the plaintiff must show that (1) she was engaged in a protected activity as defined by the Act, (2) the defendant discharged her, and (3) a causal connection exists between the protected activity and the discharge. *See* Mich. Comp. Laws Ann. § 15.362 (West 2004); *Schmidli v. City of Fraser*, 784 F.2d 794, 801 (E.D. Mich. 2011); *Whitman v. City of Burton*, 831 N.W.2d 223, 229 (Mich. 2013); *Chandler v. Dowell Schlumberger Inc.*, 57 2 N.W.2d 210, 212 (Mich. 1998). Neither party disputes that Knox was discharged or that FDA is a public body. The remaining issues are whether Knox can prove she

---

Traditionally, a sentence should not end with a preposition. You could just say "was difficult." Ch. 10.5P

Facts conclude by stating the purpose of the memo (i.e., what the client wants to know).

The first two paragraphs act as a roadmap of the controlling law and analysis. They succinctly summarize how whistleblower claims are tried and the elements of such a claim, dismiss the second element as not at issue, and prepare the reader for the analysis of the first and third elements at issue (without the writer having to explain what she is about to do). Ch. 10.3F

This citation indicates that these elements have not changed under Michigan law over time and that at least one federal court has construed the statute.

was engaged in a protected activity and whether she was fired because of her threat to report to the FDA.

The first element requires that Knox prove she was "about to" report a violation or suspected violation of law to a public body. § 15.362; *Shallal v. Catholic Soc. Servs.,* 566 N.W.2d 571, 579 (Mich. 1997). Unlike in other states the Michigan legislature chose to protect conscientious employees who intend to report but are fired before they have a chance. *Id.* at 575. About to report means "on the verge of" doing so. *Id.* In cases construing the WPA, the United States District Court for the Eastern District of Michigan has said that a plaintiff must prove that she was about to report, verbally or in writing, and 2) that the person who fired her was "objectively aware" that she was about do report before she was fired. *See, e.g., Schmidli,* 784 F.2d at 801; *see also Kaufman & Payton, P.C. v. Nikkila,* 503 N.W.2d 728, 732 (Mich. Ct. App. 1993) (noting a defendant's right to objective notice of a report or a threat to report by a whistleblower). This must be shown by clear and convincing evidence. *Id.*

In *Shallal,* an employee of a social service agency told her supervisor that she was going to report his misuse of agency funds to the Department of Social Services if he did not "straighten up." In addition to making the threat, she discussed her plan to report her supervisor with her co-workers and a member of her employer's Board of Directors. In a suit against her supervisor under the WPA, the court noted that the plaintiff had discussed reporting with third parties, but it held that the express threat to report—made directly to her supervisor—was sufficient. *Id.* at 579. In this case, Knox confronted Betz and explicitly told her she would report her to the FDA if she gave Knox any more potentially tainted blood. That threat was communicated directly to Kleusing via Betz. Kleusing was thus "objectively aware" that Knox was about to report.

The topic sentence indicates this paragraph will begin the discussion of the first element. Note the writer could have included her prediction here as well. Ch. 7.1.C.ii, p. 129.

Comma needed after "other states," because these words complete an introductory phrase to the sentence. Ch. 10.5E

This paragraph includes a general and synthesized rule (the major premise) on "about to" report. Note that it took several sentences to explain this complex rule. That's fine. It also uses an explanatory parenthetical to add authority without length. Ch. 10.3K

This paragraph begins an explanation of the rule from *Shallal;* it explains the key facts, holding, and reasoning of the court in that case.

Em dashes can be used for emphasis. Ch. 10.4N

The last two sentences of this paragraph state the facts of Knox's case (the minor premise) and analogize Knox's case to *Shallal.*

Cases where plaintiffs have failed to establish they were about to report are likely distinguishable. In some cases, the plaintiff failed to make an actual threat. *See, e.g. Schmidli*, 784 F. Supp. 2d at 801 (holding that the plaintiff's collected documentation, inquiries to public bodies, and disagreements with her supervisor did not amount to a threat). In other cases, the plaintiff failed to make the threat known to the supervisor, or the supervisor denied a threat was ever made and there was no corroborating evidence of the threat. *See, e.g., Richards v. Sandusky Cmty. Schs.*, 102 F. Supp. 2d 753, 760 (E.D. Mich. 2000) (holding that plaintiff's concerns and intent to report were not known to the defendant as required under the WPA); *Hays v. Lutheran Soc. Servs.*, 832 N.W.2d 433, 438 (Mich. Ct. App. 2013) (holding the plaintiff was not "about to report" when she told no one about her intent to report); *Pope v. Brinks Home Sec. Co.*, Nos. 294600 & 294609, 2011 WL 711133, at *7 (Mich. Ct. App. March 1, 2011) (holding the plaintiff was not "about to" report when the defendant denied she made the alleged threat and no one else had allegedly heard it). In this case, Betz communicated the threat directly to Kleusing, who does not dispute having been aware of it.

As part of the first element, Knox must also prove that she was about to report a "suspected violation" because she had been told that the refrigerator used to store the blood was functioning properly. *See* § 15.362; *Melchi v. Burns Int'l Sec. Serv., Inc.*, 597 F. Supp. 575, 583 (E.D. Mich. 1984). A suspected violation is behavior that an employee, acting in good faith, reasonably believes is against the law. *Smith v. Gentiva Health Serv. Inc.*, 296 F. Supp. 2d 758, 762 (E.D. Mich. 2003); *Melchi*, 597 F. Supp. at 583–84. In *Melchi*, a security guard of a nuclear facility observed the defendant destroy and falsify security records. Although the plaintiff could not establish that this behavior violated any law, the court held the guard had acted in good faith and his belief was reasonable because of "the pervasive regulation of the nuclear power industry by state and federal agencies." *Melchi*, 597 F. Supp. at 583–84.

In this paragraph, the writer anticipates the defendant's counter-arguments by distinguishing cases where the plaintiff failed to establish "about to" report. Notice the writer anticipates the defendant's arguments without having to say "the defendant may claim" or "the defendant may cite." Ch. 7.1–7.2

Having examined the potential counter-arguments, the writer concludes on this sub-issue.

Topic sentence here indicates the writer is transitioning to the second sub-issue under the first element. She includes a synthesized rule on "suspected violation" that explains the element and how it has been interpreted.

The writer states the synthesized rule (major premise) for "suspected violation."

Explanation of the rule with key facts, holding, and court's reasoning.

Like in *Melchi*, Knox likely acted in good faith and her belief was likely reasonable. The healthcare industry is as highly regulated as the nuclear power industry, and the FDA has strict regulations relating to blood storage. Thus, Knox could reasonably believe it was unlawful to use blood she thought had been stored improperly. Unlike the security guard in *Melchi*, who was certain that the defendant had destroyed documents, Knox was not certain that the refrigerator was malfunctioning. However, in view of the health risks to patients from contaminated blood and Knox's experience, a Michigan court is likely to hold that Knox acted in good faith and with a reasonable belief of a "suspected violation."

Analogy to Melchi.

The writer anticipates how the hospital might try to distinguish Melchi.

Conclusion.

To prove the third element, that a causal connection exists between the protected activity and Knox's discharge, Knox must show a causal, not just a temporal, connection between her protected activity and her termination. *See West v. Gen. Motors Co.*, 665 N.W.2d 468, 473 (Mich. Ct. App. 2003); *Taylor v. Modern Eng'g, Inc.*, 653 N.W.2d 625, 630 (Mich. Ct. App. 2002); *Roulston v. Tendercare, Inc.*, 608 N.W.2d 525, 530 (Mich. Ct. App. 2000). However, the burden of establishing a prima facie case is not intended to be onerous. If a reasonable juror could conclude that Knox would not have been fired if she had not threatened to report, the causal requirement is met. *West*, 665 N.W.2d at 473 (stating that a whistleblower plaintiff must show the adverse action "was in some manner influenced by the protected activity"); *cf. Nguyen v. City of Cleveland*, 229 F.3d 559, 563 (6th Cir. 2000) (discussing the causal connection in a failure to promote case under Title VII). In *Roulston,* the plaintiff, a social services director at a nursing home, was fired within hours of reporting suspected abuse to state regulators. The court held that the extent of her supervisor's anger, his harsh language, his watching her collect her belongings, and her performance record suggested the plaintiff had been fired because she had reported. *Roulston*, 608 N.W.2d at 530. The court also noted that if the defendant could establish a legitimate reason for the discharge, the plaintiff

This topic sentence transitions the reader from the first to the third element and reminds the reader what the third element is.

Here, the writer explains the synthesized rule on causal connection.

This paragraph explains how the rule was applied in Roulston.

would have an opportunity to show that the defendant's stated reason was a pretext, and pretext can be shown even where the defendant acts from mixed motives (e.g., both a legitimate and a retaliatory reason). *Id; see also Melchi*, 597 F. Supp. at 583.

Like Roulston, Knox is likely to establish a causal connection between her threat to report and her discharge. First, Knox was also fired soon after she threatened to report, roughly one week later, even though she had worked at the hospital for roughly five years. Second, like Roulston's supervisor, Betz's reaction to Knox's concerns was anger, which she would have communicated to Kleusing, who fired her. Finally, Knox's performance record—she was reprimanded just one in five years—suggests her threat to report motivated Kleusing, at least in part, to fire her. As long as the threat to report contributed to Knox being discharged, she is likely to prove causation.

> The writer compares Knox's case (the minor premise) to *Roulston.* She also explains that once a prima facie claim is established, Knox can likely establish pretext.

> The writer states her conclusion on the third element.

Conclusion

Knox is likely to succeed in her whistleblower claim against the hospital under Michigan's Whistleblowers' Protection Act. Knox's threat to Betz, who conveyed it to Kleusing, establishes that Knox was "about to" report. There is no indication that either Betz or Kleusing will deny those statements. Because the storage of blood for hospital use is highly regulated by the FDA, Knox can also establish that she acted in good faith and reasonably believed that Betz's use of potentially tainted blood was against the law. Finally, Knox can probably prove that a causal connection exists between her threat to report and her discharge. In addition to Knox being discharged within just one week of the threat, both Betz and Kleusing were upset about the threat, and Knox had an excellent performance record. For these reasons, any reason the defendant states for firing Knox is likely to be considered a pretext.

> The conclusion recaps for the reader how the writer reached her conclusion, explaining why she believes Knox will succeed in proving the disputed elements of the claim.

APPENDIX D

EXCERPTS FROM APPELLATE BRIEFS IN *TEXAS BEEF GROUP V. WINFREY*[1]

■ ■ ■

A major issue in this case was whether live cattle could be considered a perishable food product under the Texas false disparagement statute. A group of cattle ranchers sued Oprah Winfrey, who had hosted an episode of her talk show in Texas on the subject of mad cow disease. The plaintiffs sued Winfrey for several causes of action, one of which was false disparagement. These briefs are here to give you a sense of how differently these issues can be presented and argued from each client's perspective. They are good, not perfect, and you will see punctuation, citation and other sorts of mechanical errors.

EXCERPTS FROM APPELLANT'S BRIEF

Statement of the issue presented for review

Whether the district court erred in granting Defendants Motion for Judgment as a Matter of Law with respect to whether cattle are perishable pursuant to Chapter 96 of the Texas Civil Practice and Remedies Code.

. . .

Argument (excerpt)

DEFENDANTS MOTION FOR JUDGMENT AS A MATTER OF LAW WITH RESPECT TO WHETHER CATTLE ARE PERISHABLE WITHIN THE MEANING OF CHAPTER 96.

A. **Federal Rule of Civil Procedure 50(a) Standard of Review and Applicable Law.**

A motion for Judgment as a Matter of Law is no different than a summary judgment motion and the appellate court applies the same standard as the district court. "The primary difference is procedural; summary judgment motions are usually made before trial and decided on documentary evidence, while directed verdict motions are made at trial and decided on the evidence that has been admitted. . . . In essence, though, the inquiry under each is the same . . ." *Anderson v. Liberty Lobby, Inc.,* 106 S.Ct. 2505, 2512 (1986). The appellate court applies a de novo standard of review.

---

[1]   201 F.3d 680 (5th Cir. 2000).

See e.g. *Estate of Bonner v. United States*, 84 F.3d 196 (5th Cir. 1996). Accordingly, a motion for Judgment as a Matter of Law should be denied unless the movant proves that there is no genuine issue of material fact and that the moving party is entitled to Judgment as a Matter of Law. *See* e.g., *Grillet v. Sears Roebuck & Co.*, 927 F.2d 220 (5th Cir. 1991).

In determining a motion for Judgment as a Matter of Law, courts view the facts in the light most favorable to the nonmovant and give the nonmovant the advantage of fair and reasonable inferences from the facts. *Texas Farm Bureau v. United States*, 53 F.3d 120, 123 (5th Cir. 1995); *Woodall v. City of El Paso*, 49 F.3d 1120, 1124 (5th Cir. 1995). Consequently, the burden is "heavy" on the party seeking a Rule 50(a) Judgment as a Matter of Law. *Paz v. Sherwin-Williams*, 917 F. Supp. 51, 52 (D.D.C. 1996). In order for the district court to properly grant such a motion, it must find that the facts and reasonable inferences point so strongly and overwhelmingly in favor of the moving party that "reasonable persons could not arrive at a contrary verdict . . ." *Texas Farm Bureau*, 53 F.3d at 123; *Woodall,*, 49 F.3d at 1124. In other words, the evidence and the inferences therefrom must so strongly favor the movant, that *no* jury could decide in favor of the nonmovant. *Walter v. Holiday Inns, Inc.*, 985 F.2d 1232, 1238 (3d Cir. 1993); *accord, Paz, supra* (The Court must deny Rule 50(a) motions " 'where fair-minded people *might* differ as to' the appropriate verdict (citation omitted)."

B. Cattle Are Perishable Within the Meaning of Chapter 96, Texas Civil Practice and Remedies Code § 96.001 et seq. ("False Disparagement of Perishable Foods Act").

1. Perishability as Defined in Chapter 96

Texas Civil Practice and Remedies Code Chapter 96 is the Texas False Disparagement of Perishable Foods Act.[18] A perishable food is defined as an agricultural product distributed in a form that will "perish or decay beyond marketability within a limited period of time." Tex. Civ. Prac. & Rem. Code § 96.001 (Vernon Supp. 1996). Section 96.002 provides liability for persons

---

[18]   Texas produces almost twenty-five percent of the fed beef consumed in the U.S., more than is produced by any other state. Plaintiff's Cactus Feeders, Inc. and Cactus Growers, Inc. are among the largest beef producers in the world. In the mid-90's, the Texas legislature recognized that food producers such as the Plaintiffs are particularly vulnerable to "the careless or malicious use of false or misleading information and the subsequent market effect." House Comm. On Agriculture and Livestock, Bill Analysis, Tex. H.B. 722, 74th Leg. The legislature's concern was prompted by the Alar apple scare that cost apple growers in Washington State more than $125 million. The Alar scare resulted from a *60 Minutes* broadcast that contained sensationalized allegations linking Alar to cancer. It was later discovered that the disseminators of these damaging allegations had no recognized scientific data to validate the charges. But it was too late, the damage had been done. Family apple producers that had thrived for generations were put out of business as fear consumed the marketplace. Accordingly, the legislature amended the Texas Civil Practice and Remedies Code to ensure that "claims about the health, safety and wholesomeness" of food produced in Texas "are based on reasonable reliable scientific data, not sensationalized claims made by groups or individuals seeking publicity for their agendas." House Comm. On Agriculture and Livestock, Bill Analysis, Tex. H.B. 722, 74th Leg. (Tex. 1996).

who knowingly disseminate false information about a perishable food product:

(a)   A person is liable as provided by Subsection (b) if:

(1)   The person disseminates in any manner information relating to a perishable food product to the public;

(2)   The person knows the information is false; and

(3)   The information states or implies that the perishable food product is not safe for consumption by the public.

(b)   A person who is liable under Subsection (a) is liable to the producer of the perishable food product for damages and any other appropriate relief arising from the person's dissemination of the information.

In determining if information is false, the trier of fact shall consider whether the information was based on reasonable and reliable scientific inquiry, facts, or data.

Tex. Civ. Prac. & Rem. Code §§ 96.002 and 96.003 (Vernon Supp. 1996).

In granting defendants' Rule 50(a) motions, the district court held that "[l]ive fed cattle [do not] fit within the carefully crafted statutory language which requires that the food product in question perish or decay 'beyond marketability'". (Doc. 550 in Case No. 2–96–CV–208; RE tab number 8). The Court concluded that there is no legally sufficient evidentiary basis for a reasonable jury to find that Plaintiffs produce a food product that will perish or decay beyond marketability within a limited period of time." The district court's analysis and conclusion is wrong.

Ample evidence was introduced during Plaintiffs' case-in-chief that the beef[19] produced by the Plaintiffs is a perishable food that "is sold or distributed in a form that will perish or decay beyond marketability within a limited period of time."[20] See, e.g., Tr. at 264 ("cattle are a perishable product"), 780 ("[cattle are] in a form that could perish or decay beyond marketability within a very short period of time"); See also, Tr. at 784, 785, and 786). The plaintiffs also presented evidence that they "grow" cattle, produce finished cattle, sell their fed cattle to the slaughterhouse, and receive payment based on the meat.[21]

Plaintiffs introduced evidence in their case-in-chief that fed cattle are like fruit or produce in that they must be marketed within a very narrow

---

[19]   The defendants did not, and could not, argue that beef is not perishable. See House Research Organization, Bill Analysis of CSHB 722 at p. 16. (False disparagement of perishable food product statute "would help ensure that any claim about the safety of . . . meat . . . is based on facts.").

[20]   During the *defendants* case-in-chief (after the Court made its ruling), one of the defendants expert witnesses, Dr. Marvin Hayenga, testified that the plaintiffs' beef is a perishable food product. (*See* Tr. At 5092).

[21]   *See*, e.g. Tr. at 489, 1138, 3175, 3181, 3190, 3467, 3566, and 3713; *See also*, e.g. Tr. at 258, 264, 548, 780, 784, 785, 786, 797, 888, 3187, 3497, 3566, 3607, 3713, 4253, and 5180.

window of time or they will "perish or decay." (*See, e.g.,* Tr. at 780, 781). Although fed cattle mature at varying ages and weights depending upon genetics, each group of similar fed cattle have an ideal marketing weight. (*See, e.g.* Tr. at 622, 783, 784, and 884). Once the fed cattle have achieved the desired and optimum marketing or "finished" weight, they begin to add fat instead of muscle. (*See, e.g.* Tr. at 622, 3349, 3428, and 3497). Fed cattle must be marketed within a limited window of time, which opens after they have achieved their "finished" weight and closes when they begin to accumulate fat which causes their value and marketability to diminish rapidly and dramatically. (*See, e.g.,* Tr. at 622, 884, 3349, 3428, and 3497). This is because consumers buy certain sized pieces of beef with certain characteristics. (Tr. at 785). Like fruit that is too ripe, or vegetables that are too soft, consumers do not buy beef that is too tough and/or heavily laden with fat. (Tr. at 622).[22]

It is clear that Plaintiffs introduced legally sufficient evidence in their case-in-chief for a reasonable jury to find that fed cattle are a perishable food product and subject to the protection afforded by Chapter 96. They are sold or distributed in a form that will perish or decay beyond marketability within a limited period of time, and are exactly the type of food products the legislature sought to protect with Chapter 96.

The legislative history of Chapter 96 further demonstrates that the district court improperly analyzed and applied the statute in this case. During the hearings to consider the enactment of the statutory scheme, all of the major cattle associations in Texas testified about the need to protect the marketability of cattle from false and disparaging information. The legislature concluded that enacting Chapter 96 would "help ensure that any claim made about the safety of perishable fruits, vegetables, *meat*, cheese and other food products is based on facts . . . Special interest groups have a vested interest—sometimes motivated for their need for publicity—in keeping the public agitated about the safety of food products. The willingness of the news media to disseminate sensational claims about food safety, without investigating the claims, has hurt the agriculture industry. The public tends to believe news reports and often cannot distinguish between scientific fact and hearsay." House Comm. On Agriculture and Livestock, Bill Analysis, Tex. H.B. 722, 74th Leg. (Tex. 1996) (emphasis added).

The Texas legislature recognized that food producers in Texas are vulnerable to the malicious use of false or misleading information especially "considering the short amount of time available to harvest and market

---

[22] The Court's conclusion that fed cattle are not entitled to protection under Chapter 96 because a cattle feeder can market the perished or decayed beef to *some* buyer is illogical and vitiates the intent of the statute. Testimony was introduced that if a producer were to keep cattle until it decayed or perished, the only market for his product would be with the producers of *dog food.* (Tr. at 3350). When a cattle feeder is forced to sell his product to a producer of dog food, he or she clearly is not marketing the product to the intended consumer. The Court's analysis would preclude, for example, a strawberry, banana, or tomato producer from seeking the protection of Chapter 96 since conceivably they could dispose of their rotten produce to drug and vitamin manufacturers who produce penicillin or potassium. Clearly this is not the intent of Chapter 96.

perishable agricultural ... food products."[23] Moreover, in enacting the statutory scheme, the Texas legislature sought to protect cattle feeders such as the Plaintiffs when they concluded that "it can be difficult to recover damages for disparaged crops that have not been harvested."[24]

The legislative history demonstrates that the statutory scheme was designed to protect agricultural products before they are harvested as well as after harvest. Just as much as an apple grower holds apples on a tree before harvest, the plaintiffs hold beef in the form of fed cattle before "harvest."

Applying the standard of review to the arguments presented at the district court and herein, there was at least a genuine issue of material fact that fair-minded people *might* differ as to whether cattle are perishable within the meaning of Chapter 96. *Texas Farm Bureau,* 53 F.3d at 123; *Woodall,* 49 F.3d at 1124; *Paz,* 917 F. Supp. at 52. Accordingly, the district court should have denied the defendants motion for Judgment as a Matter of Law and submitted the issues to the jury. This Court should reverse and remand plaintiffs cause of action pursuant to Texas Civil Practice and Remedies Code § 96.001 et seq. for a trial on the merits.

EXCERPTS FROM APPELLEE'S BRIEF

Statement of the issue presented for review

Was the district court correct in granting judgment as a matter of law to Appellees, with respect to Appellants' attempted cause of action under Texas Civil Practice & Remedies Code, § 96.002, because Appellants' product, cattle, is not covered by such statute, which applies only to "a perishable food product"—i.e., "a food product ... that is sold or distributed in a form that will perish or decay beyond marketability within a limited period of time"?

. . .

Argument (excerpt)

II. *The district court was correct in granting judgment as a matter of law that Appellants take nothing from Appellees on Appellants' cause of action under Texas Civil Practice & Remedies Code § 96.002 because Appellants' claim is not covered by such statute.*

A. *Texas Civil Practice & Remedies Code § 96.002 and the district court's holdings.*

Appellants sought to maintain a cause of action under Texas Civil Practice & Remedies Code § 96.002, which reads, in full, as follows:

[omitted, see on p. 287.]

------

23   Full History—HB 722, Bill Analysis, Committee Report.

24   House Research Organization, Bill Analysis of CSHB 722 at p. 17.

Texas Civil Practice & Remedies Code, § 96.001 defines the term "perishable food product" as follows:

> In this chapter, "perishable food product" means a food product of agriculture or aquaculture that is sold or distributed in a form that will perish or decay beyond marketability within a limited period of time.

Thus, § 96.002 only applies to a product that (1) is a food product and (2) is sold or distributed in a form that will perish or decay beyond marketability within a limited period of time. Moreover, even if the product is covered by the statute, the producer has no cause of action unless (1) the information disseminated by the defendant concerning the product is false and (2) the defendant knows it is false.

At the close of Appellants' case, the district court granted judgment as a matter of law to Appellees, defendants, on Appellants', plaintiffs', attempted cause of action under § 96.002. (R. Vol. 49, p. 11516). The court held that Appellants' proof had failed to show that their cattle are covered by the statute (because there is no evidence their cattle were in a form that will perish or decay "beyond marketability" within a limited period of time) and had failed to show that Appellants had a cause of action under the statute (because there is no evidence that the statements on the Program of which Appellants complain were known by Appellees to be false). (R. Vol. 49, pp. 11522–24). Either holding will support the judgment as a matter of law; Appellees submit that both holdings were correct. Moreover, Appellees will present additional grounds entitling them to judgment as a matter of law on account of Appellants' failure to prove other elements of their § 96.002 cause of action. Finally, Appellants will show that, by virtue of a jury finding and undisputed evidence, any possible error in such judgment is harmless.[6]

B.   *The district court correctly held that Texas Civil Practice & Remedies Code § 96.002, does not apply to Appellants' action for damages for the alleged diminution in the value of their cattle.*

The district court ruled that Appellants' cattle are not covered by § 96.002 because they are not a product that will perish or decay "beyond marketability" within a limited period of time. The court accepted Appellants' argument that there is an "optimal time" for fed cattle to be marketed to the slaughterer, and that, if held at the feed lot beyond that time, they will become fatter and of lesser quality and perhaps their feed cost will exceed the price obtained for additional pounds gained. However, the court concluded:

> None of this is evidence that live fed cattle fit within the carefully crafted statutory language which requires that the food product in question perish or decay "beyond marketability." The cattle in question are still marketable, although they may be less profitable,

---

[6]   As this Court stated in *Foreman v. Babcock & Wilcox Co.*, 117 F.3d 800, 804 (5th Cir. 1997), *cert. den.*, 118 S.Ct. 1050 (1998), affirming a judgment as a matter of law, "We must affirm a judgment of the district court if the result is correct, even if our affirmance is upon grounds not relied upon by the district court."

and in some cases not marketable to every buyer. Even assuming
but not deciding that live cattle are a food product, Plaintiffs do not
produce a food product that will perish or decay *beyond
marketability* within a limited period of time.

(R. Vol. 49, p. 11523, emphasis the court's).

Appellants' response to this holding is to argue that the "value and
marketability" of cattle being held for slaughter will "diminish rapidly and
dramatically" if the cattle are not sold when, or promptly after, they have
achieved their finished weight. (Brief for Appellants p. 31). In other words, it
is Appellants' position that rapid and dramatic diminution of market value is
equivalent to "beyond marketability," or, at least, a jury could so find.
However, the construction of the statutory term, "beyond marketability," is a
question of law for the court, not an issue of fact for the jury or a subject of
testimony for a witness, *Johnson v. City of Fort Worth*, 774 S.W.2d 653, 655–
56 (Tex. 1989), and in this case the district court was correct in its
construction of the statute and in declining to accept the construction posited
by Appellants. Contrary to Appellants' position, the statute does not say it
applies if the product's value will diminish below the optimum, or even below
a fair price; it says the product must be one that will perish or decay "beyond
marketability." The words "beyond" and "marketability" are not ambiguous.
A marketable product is defined as one that is "fit to be offered for sale in a
market," is "wanted by purchasers." *Garman v. Conoco, Inc.*, 886 P.2d 652,
660 n.26 (Colo. 1994). There is no evidence that fed cattle will decline, in a
limited time, to a point where they are unfit for market and no one wants
them. To the contrary, Appellant Engler himself agreed in his testimony that
"there's always a market for your live cattle." (R. Vol. 71, p. 3436). Nor did
Appellants' cattle in fact depreciate "beyond marketability" as a result of The
Oprah Winfrey Show. According to Appellants' figures, the price of cattle
declined from $61.90 per hundredweight in the week just before the Program
to a low of $55.72 two weeks after the Program and then rose to former levels
by July 5. (R. Vol. 70, pp. 3210–3218, p. 3250; PL Ex. 3565, 2060A). There is
no evidence or claim, however, that any of Appellants' cattle became unfit for
market or were left unsold. In fact, Appellants' evidence, from their own
expert, is that, during the period for which they claim damages on account of
the Program, Appellants sold more than 25 million pounds of heifers and 96
million pounds of steer. (Pl. Ex. 2064A, 2067A).

In the footnote on p. 31 of their brief, Appellants state, "Testimony was
introduced that if a producer were to keep cattle until it decayed or perished,
the only market for his product would be with the producers of *dog food*."
(emphasis Appellants'). In the testimony to which Appellants refer, the
witness, Appellant Engler, stated that cattle would be marketable for dog
food if they were kept on feed "for two or three months" past the marketing
period; he went on to say that cattle kept for one month would have to be sold
at a $200.00 a head discount but "[p]robably not for dog food." (R. Vol. 70, pp.
3350–3351). In any event, whether selling cattle for dog food constitutes a
depreciation "beyond marketability" is not before this Court in this case. As

shown on page 29 hereof, Appellants only complain that the price for the cattle sold had declined by, at most, eleven percent. (Pl. Ex. 3565, 2060A). They have not even alleged that any of the cattle which, they say, were sold at a diminished price on account of the Program, were sold for dog food; Appellant Engler testified that he has never marketed cattle for dog food. (R. Vol. 70, p. 3351.)

The trial court thus correctly held that Appellants' claim under § 96.002 lacks the essential element that their cattle will perish or decay "beyond marketability" within a limited period of time. This holding of the district court, in and of itself, supports the court's judgment as a matter of law that Appellants take nothing on their § 96.002 claim.

Should the Court need to consider the § 96.002 claim further, however, there is an additional reason why § 96.002 does not apply to this case: the statute only covers damages to a "perishable food product," and Appellants' cattle are not a "food product" nor are they "perishable." Cattle are not food; they are livestock. This distinction is recognized in federal and Texas law. In the Packers and Stockyards Act, 1921, Congress has defined "livestock" and "meat food products" as follows:

> (3) The term "meat food products" means all products and by-products of the slaughtering and meat-packing industry—if edible;

> (4) The term "livestock" means cattle, sheep, swine, horses, mules, or goats—whether live or dead;

7 U.S.C. § 182. Similarly, in the Texas Meat and Poultry Inspection Act, the following definitions are included:

> (11) "Livestock" means cattle, sheep, swine, goats, horses, mules, other equines, poultry, domestic rabbits, exotic animals, or domesticated game birds.

> (13) "Meat food product" means a product that is capable of use as human food and that is made in whole or in part from meat or other portion of the carcass of livestock. . . .

Texas Health & Safety Code § 433.003. Moreover, for § 96.002 to apply, the product not only must be a food product, it must be in a form "for consumption by the public," Texas Civil Practice & Remedies Code § 96.002(a)(3). Also, this consumable food product must be "perishable," and tend to "perish or decay." Those terms are not suggestive of live cattle. Cattle held beyond their finished weight may command a lesser price, but Appellants do not contend that they will die or become *32 rotten.[7]

Therefore, since they are not a "food product" but are livestock, and since they are not "perishable" but simply diminish in value, Appellants' cattle are

---

[7] The difference between a perishable asset and one that declines in value is noted in the Uniform Commercial Code, which requires notification of the sale of collateral unless the collateral "is perishable *or* threatens to decline speedily in value." Texas Business & Commerce Code, § 9.504(c), emphasis added.

not a "perishable food product" as required by § 96.002. Accordingly, Appellees were entitled to judgment as a matter of law, as rendered by the district court, that Appellants' cattle are not covered by § 96.002.

APPENDIX E

BIBLIOGRAPHY

■ ■ ■

Articles

Linda L. Berger, *A Revised View of the Judicial Hunch*, 10 LEGAL COMM. & RHETORIC: J. ALWD 1 (2013).

Linda L. Berger, *Applying New Rhetoric to Legal Discourse: The Ebb and Flow of Reader and Writer, Text and Context*, 49 J. LEGAL EDUC. 155 (1999).

Linda Berger, *How Embedded Knowledge Structures Affect Judicial Decision Making: An Analysis of Metaphor, Narrative, and Imagination in Child Custody Disputes*, 18 S. CAL. INTERDISC. L.J. 259 (2009).

Linda L. Berger, *The Lady, or the Tiger? A Field Guide to Metaphor and Narrative*, 50 WASHBURN L. J. 275 (2011).

Ann E. Berthoff, *From Problem-Solving to a Theory of Imagination*, 33 C. ENGLISH 636 (1972).

Lloyd F. Bitzer, *The Rhetorical Situation*, 1 PHILOSOPHY & RHETORIC 1 (1968).

Patricia Bizzell, *Cognition, Convention, and Certainty: What We Need to Know About Writing*, 3 PRE/TEXT 213 (1982).

Guido Calabresi & A. Douglas Melamed, *Property Rules, Liability Rules, and Inalienability: One View of the Cathedral*, 85 HARV. L. REV. 1089 (1972).

Guido Calabresi & Jon T. Hirschoff, *Toward a Test for Strict Liability in Torts*, 81 YALE L.J. 1055 (1972).

Kenneth D. Chestek, *The Plot Thickens: The Appellate Brief as Story*, 14 J. LEG. WRITING 127, 140–41 (2008).

Kimberlé Crenshaw, *Demarginalizing the Intersection of Race and Sex: A Black Feminist Critique of Antidiscrimination Doctrine, Feminist Theory and Antiracist Politics*, 1989 U. CHI. LEGAL F. 139 (1989).

Kimberlé Crenshaw, *Mapping the Margins: Intersectionality, Identity Politics, and Violence Against Women of Color*, 43 STANFORD L. REV. 1241 (1993).

Clare Dalton, *Where We Stand: Observations on the Situation of Feminist Legal Thought*, 3 BERKELEY WOMEN'S L.J. 1 (1988).

Harold Demsetz, *Toward a Theory of Property Rights*, 57 AM. ECON. ASS'N 347 (1967).

Christy DeSanctis, *Narrative Reasoning and Analogy: The Untold Story*, 9 LEGAL COMM. & RHETORIC: J. ALWD 149 (2012).

Linda H. Edwards, *The Convergence of Analogical and Dialectic Imaginations in Legal Discourse*, 20 LEG. STUD. F. 7 (1996).

Robert C. Ellickson, *Property in Land*, 102 Yale L.J. 1315 (1993).

Lucinda M. Finley, *Transcending Equality Theory: A Way Out of the Maternity and the Workplace Debate*, 86 COLUM. L. REV. 1118 (1986).

Brian Foley & Ruth Anne Robbins, *Fiction 101: A Primer for Lawyers on How to Use Fiction Writing Techniques to Write Persuasive Facts Sections*, 32 RUTGERS L. J. 459 (2001).

Judith D. Fischer, *Bareheaded and Barefaced Counsel: Courts React to Unprofessionalism in Lawyers' Papers*, 31 SUFFOLK U. L. REV. 1 (1997).

Lawrence M. Friedman, *The Law and Society Movement*, 38 STAN. L. REV. 763 (1986).

Bryan A. Garner, *Interviews with Supreme Court Justices*, 13 SCRIBES J. LEG. WRITING (2010) (on writing briefs and oral advocacy).

Jane Kent Gionfriddo, *Thinking Like A Lawyer: The Heuristics of Case Synthesis*, 40 TEX. TECH L. REV. 1 (2007).

Charles J. Goetz & Robert E. Scott, *Enforcing Promises: An Examination of the Basis of Contract*, 89 YALE L.J. 1261 (1980).

Gillian K. Hadfield, *Judicial Competence and the Interpretation of Incomplete Contracts*, 23 J. LEGAL STUD. 159 (1994).

Janet Halley, *The Politics of Injury: A Review of Robin West's Caring for Justice*, 1 UNBOUND: HARV. J. LEGAL LEFT 65, 83–84 (2005).

Richard L. Hasen, *The Efficient Duty to Rescue,* 15 INT'L REV. L. & ECON. 141 (1995).

Oliver Wendell Holmes, *The Path of the Law,* 10 HARV. L. REV. 457 (1897).

Joseph C. Hutcheson, Jr., *The Judgment Intuitive: The Function of the 'Hunch' in Judicial Decision,* 14 CORNELL L.Q. 274 (1928–29).

Pam Jenoff, *The Self-Assessed Writer: Harnessing Fiction-Writing Processes to Understand Ourselves as Legal Writers and Maximize Legal Writing Productivity,* 10 LEGAL COMM. & RHETORIC: J. ALWD 187 (2013).

Steven J. Johansen, *Was Colonel Sanders a Terrorist? An Essay on the Ethical Limits of Applied Legal Storytelling,* 7 LEGAL COMM. & RHETORIC: J. ALWD 63 (2010).

Christine Jolls, Cass R. Sunstein & Richard Thaler, *A Behavioral Approach to Law and Economics,* 50 STAN. L. REV. 1471 (1998).

Jeanne M. Kaiser, *When the Truth and Story Collide: What Legal Writers Can Learn from the Experience of Non-Fiction Writers about the Limits of Storytelling,* 16 J. LEG. WRITING 163 (2010).

Duncan Kennedy, *Cost Benefit Analysis of Entitlement Problems,* 33 STAN. L. REV. 387 (1981).

Orin S. Kerr, *How to Read a Legal Opinion: A Guide for New Law Students,* 11 Green Bag 2d 51 (2007).

Phillip C. Kissam, *Thinking (By Writing) About Legal Writing,* 40 VAND. L. REV. 135 (1987).

The Honorable Alex Kozinski, *The Wrong Stuff,* 1992 BYU L. REV. 325 (1992).

Charles Lane, *Book review: 'Failing Law Schools' by Brian Z. Tamanaha,* WASH. POST, Aug. 3, 2012.

Christopher C. Langdell, *Teaching Law as a Science,* 21 AM. L. REV. 123 (1887).

Karl N. Llewellyn, *Remarks on the Theory of Appellate Decision and the Rules or Canons About How Statutes Are to Be Construed,* 3 VAND. L. REV. 395 (1950).

Andrea A. Lunsford, *Cognitive Development and the Basic Writer*, 41 C. ENGLISH 38 (1979).

William Lutz, *Notes Toward a Description of Doublespeak (Revised)*, 13 Q. REV. DOUBLESPEAK 10 (1987).

Ellie Margolis, *Closing the Floodgates: Making Persuasive Policy Arguments in Appellate Briefs*, 62 MONT. L. REV. 59 (2001).

Mari J. Matsuda, *When the First Quail Calls: Multiple Consciousness as Jurisprudential Method*, 14 WOMEN'S RTS. L. REP. 297 (1992).

Jenny Morgan, *Feminist Theory as Legal Theory*, 16 MELB. U. L. REV. 743 (1988), *reprinted in* 1 FEMINIST LEGAL THEORY (Frances E. Olsen ed., 1995).

Laurel Currie Oates, *Leveling the Playing Field: Helping Students Succeed By Helping Them Learn to Read As Expert Lawyers*, 80 St. John's L. Rev. 227 (2006).

Herman Oliphant, *A Return to Stare Decisis*, 14 ABA J. 71 (1928).

Stephen Paskey, *The Law is Made of Stories Erasing the False Dichotomy Between Stories and Legal Rules*, 11 LEGAL COMM. & RHETORIC: J. ALWD 51 (2014).

Richard A. Posner, *What Do Judges and Justices Maximize? (The Same Thing Everyone Else Does)*, 3 SUP. CT. ECON. REV. 1 (1993).

Christopher Rideout & Jill Ramsfield, *Legal Writing: A Revised View*, 69 WASH. L. REV. 35 (1994).

David T. Ritchie, *The Centrality of Metaphor in Legal Analysis and Communication: An Introduction*, 58 MERCER L. REV. 839 (2007).

Ruth Anne Robbins, *Harry Potter, Ruby Slippers, and Merlin: Telling the Client's Story Using the Characters and Paradigms of the Archetypal Hero's Journey*, 29 SEATTLE U. L. REV. 767 (2006).

Ann C. Scales, *The Emergence of Feminist Jurisprudence: An Essay*, 95 YALE L.J. 1373 (1986).

Louis B. Schwartz, *With Gun and Camera Through Darkest CLS-Land*, 36 STAN. L. REV. 413 (1984).

David Segal, *Is Law School A Losing Game?*, N.Y. TIMES, Jan. 9, 2011.

David Segal, *What They Don't Teach Law Students: Lawyering*, N.Y. TIMES, Nov. 20, 2011.

Steven Shavell, *Criminal Law and the Optimal Use of Nonmonetary Sanctions as a Deterrent*, 85 COLUM. L. REV. 1232 (1985).

Michael R. Smith, *Levels of Metaphor in Persuasive Legal Writing*, 58 MERCER L. REV. 919 (2007).

Donald Stewart, *Some History Lessons for Composition Teachers*, 3 RHETORIC REV. 134 (1985).

Cass R. Sunstein, Commentary, *On Analogical Reasoning*, 106 HARV. L. REV. 741 (1993).

Kristen K. Robbins (now Robbins-Tiscione), *The Inside Scoop: What Federal Judges Really Think About the Way Lawyers Write*, 8 J. LEG. WRIT. INST. 257 (2002).

Kristen K. Robbins, *Paradigm Lost: Recapturing Classical Rhetoric to Validate Legal Reasoning*, 27 VT. LAW REV. 483 (2003).

Kristen Konrad Robbins-Tiscione, *From Snail Mail to E-Mail: Traditional Legal Memoranda in the Twenty-First Century*, 58 J. LEGAL EDUC. 32 (2008).

Jennifer Sheppard, *The "Write" Way: A Judicial Clerk's Guide to Writing for the Court*, 38 U. BALT. L. REV. 73 (2008).

Melissa H. Weresh, *Morality, Trust & Illusion: Ethos as Relationship*, 9 LEGAL COMM. & RHETORIC: J. ALWD 229 (2012).

Wendy W. Williams, *The Equality Crisis: Some Reflections on Culture, Courts, and Feminism*, 7 WOMEN'S RTS. L. REP. 175 (1981–82).

Colin E. Wrabley, *Applying Federal Court of Appeals' Precedent: Contrasting Approaches to Applying Court of Appeals' Federal Law Holdings and Erie State Law Predictions*, 3 SETON HALL CIR. REV. 1 (2006).

Books & Book Chapters

ANDREW ALTMAN, CRITICAL LEGAL STUDIES: A LIBERAL CRITIQUE 13 (1990).

RUGGERO J. ALDISERT, LOGIC FOR LAWYERS: A GUIDE TO CLEAR LEGAL THINKING (3d ed. 1997).

AMERICAN JURISPRUDENCE LEGAL FORMS 2D.

ANTOINE ARNAUD & PIERRE NICOLE, LOGIC, OR THE ART OF THINKING (Jill Vance Buroker ed., 1996).

ARISTOTLE, THE RHETORIC OF ARISTOTLE (Lane Cooper, trans., 1932).

ARISTOTLE, THE ORGANON (Harold P. Cooke & Hugh Tredennick eds., Harv. Univ. Press 1960).

ARISTOTLE, THE WORKS OF ARISTOTLE (W.D. Ross ed., Clarendon Press 1952).

GILBERT AUSTIN, CHIRONOMIA (1805).

Author Unknown, AD C. HERENNIUM (RHETORICA AD HERENNIUM) (Harry Caplan trans., Harv. Univ. Press 1954).

FRANCIS BACON, *Book 1 of the Advancement and Proficiency of Learning, in* SELECTED PHILOSOPHICAL WORKS (Rose-Mary Sargent ed., 1999).

FRANCIS BACON, SELECTED WRITINGS OF FRANCIS BACON (Hugh C. Dick ed., 1955).

FRANCIS BACON, THE NEW ORGANON (Lisa Jardine & Michael Silverthorne eds., Cambridge Univ. Press 2000) (1620).

ALEXANDER BAIN, ENGLISH COMPOSITION AND RHETORIC (Scholars' Facsimiles & Reprints 1996) (1871).

CAROL M. BALDWIN, PLAIN LANGUAGE AND THE DOCUMENT REVOLUTION (1999).

COLEEN BARGER, ALWD GUIDE TO LEGAL CITATION (5th ed. 2014).

DERRICK BELL, RACE, RACISM AND AMERICAN LAW (4th ed. 2000).

JEREMY BENTHAM, THE WORKS OF JEREMY BENTHAM (John Bowring ed., 1843).

JAMES A. BERLIN, RHETORIC AND REALITY: WRITING INSTRUCTION IN AMERICAN COLLEGES 1900–1985 (1987).

HUGH BLAIR, LECTURES ON RHETORIC AND BELLES LETTRES (1833).

THE BLUEBOOK: A UNIFORM SYSTEM OF CITATION (20th ed. 2015).

KENNETH BURKE, A RHETORIC OF MOTIVES (1950).

Steven J. Burton, An Introduction to Law and Legal Reasoning (3d ed. 2007).

George Campbell, Philosophy of Rhetoric (Charles Ewer ed., 1823).

Joseph Campbell, The Hero with a Thousand Faces (Comm. ed. 2004).

Martha Chamallas, Introduction to Feminist Legal Theory (1999).

Stuart Chase, The Power of Words (1953).

Geoffrey Chaucer, The Canterbury Tales (Jill Mann ed., Penguin Classics 2005).

Cicero, Cicero in Twenty-Eight Volumes (H.M. Hubbell trans., Harv. Univ. Press 1971).

Cicero, De Inventione (H.M. Hubbell trans., 1968) (c. 87 B.C.).

Cicero, De Oratore (E.W. Sutton trans., 1967) (c. 55 B.C.).

Cicero, Divisions of Oratory (H. Rackham trans., Harv. Univ. Press 2004).

Lane Cooper, The Rhetoric of Aristotle (1932).

Edward P.J. Corbett & Robert J. Connors, Classical Rhetoric for the Modern Student (4th ed. 1999).

Martin Cutts, The Plain English Guide (1995).

Wayne A. Davis, An Introduction to Logic (2007).

René Descartes, Discourse on Method and the Meditations (John Veitch trans., Prometheus Books 1989).

Mary L. Dunnewold, Beth A. Honetschlager, & Brenda L. Tofte, Judicial Clerkships: A Practical Guide (2010).

Linda H. Edwards, Legal Writing and Analysis (4th ed. 2015).

Peter Elbow, Writing Without Teachers (2d ed. 1998).

Encyclopedia of Rhetoric (Oxford Univ. Press 2001).

Janet Emig, The Composing Process of Twelfth Graders (1971).

ANNE ENQUIST & LAUREL CURRIE OATES, JUST WRITING: GRAMMAR, PUNCTUATION, AND STYLE FOR THE LEGAL WRITER (4th ed. 2013).

ERASMUS, DE DUPLICI COPIA VERBORUM AC RERUM (Craig R. Thompson ed., Univ. of Toronto Press 1978) (1528).

ESSAYS ON CLASSICAL RHETORIC AND MODERN DISCOURSE (Robert J. Connors et al. eds., 1984).

FEDERAL JUDICIAL CENTER, LAW CLERK HANDBOOK: A HANDBOOK FOR LAW CLERKS TO FEDERAL JUDGES (SYLVAN A. SOBEL, ED., 2D ED. 2007).

STEPHEN M. FELDMAN, AMERICAN LEGAL THOUGHT FROM PREMODERNISM TO POSTMODERNISM: AN INTELLECTUAL VOYAGE (2000).

DANIEL FOGARTY, ROOTS FOR A NEW RHETORIC (1959).

JEROME FRANK, LAW AND THE MODERN MIND (1949).

DAVID C. FREDERICK, THE ART OF ORAL ADVOCACY (2d ed. 2011).

MARY JO FRUG, POSTMODERN LEGAL FEMINISM (1992).

JAMES A. GARDNER, LEGAL ARGUMENT: THE STRUCTURE AND LANGUAGE OF EFFECTIVE ADVOCACY (1993).

BRYAN A. GARNER, LEGAL WRITING IN PLAIN ENGLISH (2001).

BRYAN A. GARNER, THE ELEMENTS OF LEGAL STYLE (2d ed. 2002).

BRYAN A. GARNER, THE REDBOOK: A MANUAL ON LEGAL STYLE (2d ed. 2006).

JOHN F. GENUNG, PRACTICAL ELEMENTS OF RHETORIC (1885).

CAROL GILLIGAN, IN A DIFFERENT VOICE: PSYCHOLOGICAL THEORY AND WOMEN'S DEVELOPMENT (1982).

JAMES L. GOLDEN ET AL., THE RHETORIC OF WESTERN THOUGHT (9th ed. 2007).

JAMES L. GOLDEN & EDWARD P.J. CORBETT, THE RHETORIC OF BLAIR, CAMPBELL, AND WHATLEY (1968).

WILLIAM GOLDMAN, ADVENTURES IN THE SCREEN TRADE: A PERSONAL VIEW OF HOLLYWOOD AND SCREENWRITING (1983).

H.L.A. HART, THE CONCEPT OF LAW (1961).

JACK HART, STORY CRAFT: THE COMPLETE GUIDE TO WRITING NARRATIVE NONFICTION (2011).

RICHARD HUGHES & ALBERT DUHAMEL, PRINCIPLES OF RHETORIC (1967).

DAVID HUME, A TREATISE OF HUMAN NATURE (David Fate Norton & Mary J. Norton eds., Oxford Univ. Press 2000).

DAVID HUME, AN ENQUIRY CONCERNING HUMAN UNDERSTANDING (Tom L. Beauchamp ed., Oxford Univ. Press 2000).

MARGARET Z. JOHNS & CLAYTON S. TANAKA, PROFESSIONAL WRITING FOR LAWYERS (2d. ed. 2012).

SISTER MIRIAM JOSEPH, THE TRIVIUM: THE LIBERAL ARTS OF LOGIC, GRAMMAR, AND RHETORIC (Marguerite McGlinn ed., Paul Dry Books 2002) (1937).

THE COLLECTED WORKS OF C. G. JUNG, ch. VII (Sir Herbert Read, Michael Fordham, & Gerhard Adler, eds. 1966).

IMMANUEL KANT, CRITIQUE OF PURE REASON 45 (F. Max Müller trans., Anchor Books 1966) (1781).

DUNCAN KENNEDY, *Legal Education as Training for Hierarchy, in* POLITICS OF LAW: A PROGRESSIVE CRITIQUE (David Kairys ed., 1982).

GEORGE A. KENNEDY, CLASSICAL RHETORIC & ITS CHRISTIAN AND SECULAR TRADITION FROM ANCIENT TO MODERN TIMES (2d ed. 1999).

JAMES L. KINNEAVY, A THEORY OF DISCOURSE (1971).

THOMAS J. KINNEY, THE COMMON TOPICS (2003–04).

WILLIAM P. LaPIANA, LOGIC & EXPERIENCE: THE ORIGIN OF MODERN AMERICAN LEGAL EDUCATION (1994).

LAW AND ECONOMICS (Jules Coleman & Jeffrey Lange eds., 1992).

Charles Lawrence III, *The Id, the Ego, and Equal Protection Reckoning with Unconscious Racism, in* CRITICAL RACE THEORY: THE KEY WRITINGS THAT FORMED THE MOVEMENT (Kimberlé Crenshaw et al. eds., 1995).

EDWARD H. LEVI, AN INTRODUCTION TO LEGAL REASONING (1949).

JOHN LOCKE, AN ESSAY CONCERNING HUMAN UNDERSTANDING (John Yolton ed., Dutton rev. ed. 1964) (1689).

ANDREA A. LUNSFORD AND JOHN J. RUSZKIEWICZ, EVERYTHING'S AN ARGUMENT (4th ed. 2007).

CATHERINE A. MACKINNON, FEMINISM UNMODIFIED: DISCOURSES ON LIFE AND LAW (1987).

RUTH ANN MCKINNEY, READING LIKE A LAWYER (2d ed. 2012).

DAVID MELLINKOFF, THE LANGUAGE OF THE LAW (1963).

PHILIP N. MEYER, STORYTELLING FOR LAWYERS (2014).

JAMES J. MURPHY, A SHORT HISTORY OF WRITING INSTRUCTION: FROM ANCIENT GREECE TO TWENTIETH CENTURY AMERICA 170 (1990).

JAMES J. MURPHY, RHETORIC IN THE MIDDLE AGES: A HISTORY OF RHETORICAL THEORY FROM SAINT AUGUSTINE TO THE RENAISSANCE (1974).

JAMES J. MURPHY & RICHARD A. KATULA, A SYNOPTIC HISTORY OF CLASSICAL RHETORIC (3d ed. 2003).

James J. Murphy, *Rhetorical History as a Guide to the Salvation of American Reading and Writing: A Plea for Curricular Courage, in* THE RHETORICAL TRADITION AND MODERN WRITING (James J. Murphy ed., 1982).

JOYCE CAROL OATES, RAPE: A LOVE STORY (2003).

THE OXFORD CLASSICAL DICTIONARY (Simon Hornblower & Antony Spawforth eds., 4th ed. 2005).

THE OXFORD COMPACT ENGLISH DICTIONARY (Catherine Soanes ed., 2d ed. 2003).

CHAIM PERELMAN, JUSTICE, LAW, AND ARGUMENT (1980).

CHAIM PERELMAN & LUCIE OLBRECHTS-TYTECA, THE NEW RHETORIC: A TREATISE ON ARGUMENTATION (1958).

CHAIM PERELMAN, THE REALM OF RHETORIC (William Kluback trans., Univ. of Notre Dame Press 1982).

LES PERELMAN, *The Medieval Art of Letter-Writing: Rhetoric as an Institutional Expression, in* TEXTUAL DYNAMICS OF THE PROFESSIONS (Charles Bazerman & James Paradis eds., 1991).

PLATO, COMPLETE WORKS (John M. Cooper ed., Hackett Pub. Co. Inc. 1997).

RICHARD A. POSNER, ECONOMIC ANALYSIS OF LAW (7th ed. 2007).

QUINTILIAN, INSTITUTIO ORATORIO (Donald A. Russell trans. & ed., Harv. Univ. Press 2001).

PETER RAMUS, LOGIKE (1574).

MARY RAY & JILL J. RAMSFIELD, LEGAL WRITING: GETTING IT RIGHT AND GETTING IT WRITTEN (5th ed. 2010).

WAYNE A. REBHORN, RENAISSANCE DEBATES ON RHETORIC (2000).

I.A. RICHARDS & C. K. OGDEN, THE MEANING OF MEANING (1923).

I.A. RICHARDS, THE PHILOSOPHY OF RHETORIC (1936).

RUTH ANNE ROBBINS, STEVE JOHANSEN, & KEN CHESTEK, YOUR CLIENT'S STORY: PERSUASIVE LEGAL WRITING (2013).

WILL ROGERS, *The Lawyers Talking, in* 6 WILL ROGERS' WEEKLY ARTICLES: THE ROOSEVELT YEARS, 1933–1935 (Steven K. Gragert ed., Will Rogers Mem'l Museums rev. ed. 2011) (1982).

CHARLES ROLLIN, THE METHOD OF TEACHING AND STUDYING THE BELLES LETTRES (A. Bettesworth & C. Hitch trans., 1734).

MARJORIE DICK ROMBAUER, LEGAL PROBLEM SOLVING: ANALYSIS, RESEARCH, AND WRITING (1991).

W. D. ROSS, ARISTOTLE'S PRIOR AND POSTERIOR ANALYTICS (Leonardo Taran ed., Garland Publishing, Inc. 1980) (1949).

ANNETTE T. ROTTENBERG, THE STRUCTURE OF ARGUMENT (3d ed. 2000).

A SELECT LIBRARY OF THE NICENE AND POST-NICENE FATHERS OF THE CHRISTIAN CHURCH: ST. AUGUSTINE'S CITY OF GOD AND CHRISTIAN DOCTRINE (Phillip Schaff, ed. 1956).

KAREN A. SCHRIVER, DYNAMICS IN DOCUMENT DESIGN (1997).

WILLIAM SHAKESPEARE, HAMLET (New Folger ed., Wash. Square Press 2003).

WILLIAM SHAKESPEARE, ROMEO AND JULIET (New Folger ed., Wash. Square Press 2004).

WILLIAM SHAKESPEARE, THE SECOND PART OF KING HENRY VI (New Folger ed., Wash. Square Press 1988).

RICHARD SHERRY, A TREATISE OF SCHEMES AND TROPES (1550).

AMY E. SLOAN, BASIC LEGAL RESEARCH: TOOLS AND STRATEGIES (2015).

MICHAEL R. SMITH, ADVANCED LEGAL WRITING: THEORIES AND STRATEGIES IN PERSUASIVE WRITING (3d ed. 2012).

DONALD C. STEWART, THE AUTHENTIC VOICE: A PRE-WRITING APPROACH TO STUDENT WRITING (1972).

ROY STUCKEY AND OTHERS, BEST PRACTICES FOR LEGAL EDUCATION: A VISION AND A ROAD MAP (2007).

WILLIAM M. SULLIVAN, ET AL., EDUCATING LAWYERS: PREPARATION FOR THE PRACTICE OF LAW 13 (2007).

JONATHAN SWIFT, THE BATTLE OF THE BOOKS (Sir Henry Craik ed., 1912).

JONATHON SWIFT, A PROPOSAL FOR CORRECTING, IMPROVING AND ASCERTAINING THE ENGLISH TONGUE (R.C. Alston ed., Scolar Press 1969) (1712).

THOMAS SHERIDAN, A COURSE OF LECTURES ON ELOCUTION (1762, reissued 1968).

BRIAN Z. TAMANAHA, FAILING LAW SCHOOLS (2011).

STEPHEN E. TOULMIN, THE USES OF ARGUMENT (Cambridge Univ. Press updated ed. 2003) (1958).

BRIAN VICKERS, IN DEFENCE OF RHETORIC (1988).

GIAMBATTISTA VICO, THE ART OF RHETORIC (Giorgio A. Pinton & Arthur W. Shippee trans. & eds., 1996) (c. 1711–44).

GIAMBATTISTA VICO, THE NEW SCIENCE OF GIAMBATTISTA VICO (Thomas Goddard Bergin & Max Harold Fisch trans., Cornell Univ. Press 3d ed. 1984) (1744).

JOHN WALKER, ELEMENTS OF ELOCUTION (R.C. Alston ed., Scolar Press 1969) (1781).

JOHN WARD, A SYSTEM OF ORATORY (1759).

MELISSA H. WERESH, LEGAL WRITING: ETHICAL AND PROFESSIONAL CONSIDERATIONS (2d ed. 2009).

WEST'S LEGAL FORMS.

RICHARD WHATELY, ELEMENTS OF RHETORIC (Douglas Ehninger ed., 1963).

JOSEPH WILLIAMS & JOSEPH BIZUP, STYLE: LESSONS IN CLARITY AND GRACE (11th ed. 2013).

THOMAS WILSON, THE ART OF RHETORIC (Peter Medine ed., Penn. State Univ. Press 1994) (1560).

CHRISTOPHER G. WREN & JILL R. WREN, THE LEGAL RESEARCH MANUAL: A GAME PLAN FOR LEGAL RESEARCH AND ANALYSIS (2d ed. 1986).

THE WRITING TEACHER'S SOURCEBOOK (Gary Tate & Edward P.J. Corbett eds., 2d ed. 1988).

- Robert J. Connors, *The Rise and Fall of the Modes of Discourse,* 32 C. COMPOSITION & COMM. 444 (1981).

- Linda Flower & John R. Hayes, *The Cognition of Discovery: Defining a Rhetorical Problem,* 31 C. COMPOSITION & COMM. 21 (1980).

- Sondra Perl, *Understanding Composing,* 31 C. COMPOSITION & COMM. 363 (1980).

- Nancy Sommers, *Revision Strategies of Student Writers and Experienced Adult Writers,* 31 C. COMPOSITION & COMM. 378 (1980).

THE WRITING TEACHER'S SOURCEBOOK (Gary Tate, Edward P.J. Corbett & Nancy Myers eds., 3d ed. 1994).

- James A. Berlin, *Contemporary Composition: The Major Pedagogical Theories,* 44 C. ENGLISH 765 (1982).

THE WRITING TEACHERS' SOURCEBOOK (Edward P.J. Corbett, Nancy Myers & Gary Tate eds., 4th ed. 2000).

- James A. Berlin, *Rhetoric and Ideology in the Writing Class,* 50 C. ENGLISH 477 (1988).

- Lisa Ede & Andrea Lunsford, *Audience Address/Audience Invoked: The Role of Audience in Composition Theory and Pedagogy,* 35 C. COMPOSITION & COMM. 55 (1984).

- James A. Reither, *Writing and Knowing: Toward Redefining the Writing Process* 47 C. ENGLISH 620 (1985).

RICHARD WYDICK, PLAIN ENGLISH FOR LAWYERS (5th ed. 2005).

RICHARD YOUNG, PARADIGMS AND PROBLEMS: SOME NEEDED RESEARCH IN RHETORICAL INVENTION, RESEARCH ON COMPOSING: POINTS OF VIEW OF DEPARTURE (Charles R. Cooper & Lee Odell eds., 1978).

Richard E. Young & Alton L. Becker, *Toward a Modern Theory of Rhetoric, reprinted in* CONTEMPORARY RHETORIC: A CONCEPTUAL BACKGROUND WITH READINGS (W. Ross Winterowd ed., 1975).

Statutes, Orders, Rules & Model Laws

Exec. Order No. 12,044, 3 C.F.R. 152 (1978).

Exec. Order No. 12,174, 3 C.F.R. 462 (1980).

FED. R. APP. P.

FED. R. CIV. P.

MODEL RULES OF PROF'L CONDUCT (2015), *available at* http://www. abanet.org/cpr/mrpc/home.html.

TEX. CIV. PRAC. & REM. CODE ANN. §§ 96.001–.004 (2011).

Names and Subjects Index

References are to Pages

ADVERBS, USE SPARINGLY, 236

"AFFECT," USE OF, 246

AGAINST THE WEIGHT OF THE
    EVIDENCE, 203

AGENCY
Decisions, 53, 57, 72–73, 203
Filings, 4
Regulations, 5, 57, 61, 69, 72–73, 82, 223–
    224

ALBERIC, 28

ALDISERT, JUDGE RUGGERIO J., 80,
    87, 95, 106

ALLEMANUS, HERMANNUS, 27

ALLITERATION, 27, 247

ALWD GUIDE TO LEGAL CITATION,
    62–63, 66, 75, 169, 213, 235–239

AMERICAN LAW REPORTS, 57

AMERICAN LEGAL REALISM, 41
See also Realism

ANALOGY OR ANALOGICAL
    REASONING, 79–80, 93, 103–109,
    233–234, 249
Burton, Steven, 95, 105–106, 108
    The judgment of importance, 105–
        106, 108, 111–112
Fallacies in analogical reasoning, 106
    The house of cards (relying on a case
        with an adverse outcome), 107
    The missing link (too much missing
        information), 106
    The problem with totality of
        circumstances tests, 108

ANALYTICAL PARADIGM, 79–80, 110,
    127, 136, 183, 209, 231

APPEALS TO ETHOS
As artistic appeal, 47
Directly adverse authority, 168
Duty of candor to the tribunal, 168
In legal advocacy, 166
In predictive writing, 117
Professional identity, as part of, 13, 170
Professionalism in legal advocacy, 170

APPEALS TO LOGOS
    See also Chapter 5, Appeals to
        Reason
As artistic appeal, 47

APPEALS TO PATHOS
As artistic appeal, 47
Framing the law from your client's
    perspective, 163
Framing your client's story, 160
In legal advocacy, 156
In predictive writing, 116
Theory of the case, 160

APPELLATE BRIEFS, 188–219 and
    Appendix D
Format, 189
    Argument, 191
    Conclusion, 191
    Cover page, 189
    Jurisdictional statement, 189
    Standard of review, 191, 202
    Statement of the case, 190
        Drafting a persuasive
            statement, 204
        Specific techniques for drafting,
            205
    Statement of the issues, 190
    Summary of argument, 190
    Table of authorities, 189
    Table of contents, 189
Organization, 206
    Headings, major, minor, and sub-,
        212
    Large-scale, 206
    Roadmaps, 214
    Small-scale, 209
Sample appellate brief, 192 and Appendix
    D

APPELLATE DECISIONS, 6

APPELLATE OPINIONS, 224

ARBITRARY AND CAPRICIOUS, 203

ARGUMENT
As type of writing, 50

ARISTOTLE, 15, 21–22, 27–28, 50
Artistic proofs, 79, 116–117, 156–157, 166
Canons of rhetoric, 47–48, 221, 255
Categorical syllogism, see Legal syllogism
ORGANON, THE, 27

Rhetoric, as part of invention, 17, 39
Syllogism, 15, 17–18, 21–22, 27–28, 30, 35,
    39, 47–52, 69–70, 79, 88–89, 92
Topics, the, 69
    Common, 70
    Special, 70

ARNAUD, FRANCOIS, 34
LOGIC OR THE ART OF THINKING, 34

ARRANGEMENT
In legal advocacy
    Briefs, appellate, 189
    Complaints, 173
    Memoranda of points and authorities,
        182
    Motions, 179
    Oral argument, 260
In predictive writing
    Bench memoranda, 147
    Email, 135
    Legal memoranda, 119
    Opinion letters, 141

ARTISTIC APPEALS, 47, 53

ASSONANCE, 247

AUGUSTINE OF HIPPO, 25, 27
CONFESSIONS, 25

AUSTIN, GILBERT, 36
CHIRONOMIA, 36

BACON, FRANCIS, 31–32, 34–35
Great Instauration, The, 31
On induction, 32
NEW ORGANON, THE, 32
Scientific method, 50
On style, 222

BAIN, ALEXANDER, 50

BASTIAN, ANDREW, 161

BEGGING THE QUESTION, 101

BELL, DERRICK, 43–44

BELLE LETTRES MOVEMENT, 31, 35–
    36
Blair, Hugh, 36, 50
    LECTURES ON RHETORIC AND BELLE
        LETTRES, 36

BELLETRISTIC
See Belle Lettres Movement

BENCH MEMORANDA, 3–4, 115–116,
    146–154
Format, 147
Sample bench memorandum, 149

BENTHAM, JEREMY, 222

BERGER, LINDA, 52, 109, 111, 251

BERLIN, JAMES, 41, 49–52

BINDING, AS AUTHORITY, 61–65, 71–
    73, 167–170

BITZER, 16, 27
Audience, 16
Constraints, 16
Exigence, 16
Rhetorical forms, 16
Rhetorical situation, 16

BIZZELL, PATRICIA, 52

BLAIR, HUGH, 36, 50

BLOOMBERG LAW, 202

BLUEBOOK, THE, 62–63, 66, 75, 169,
    213, 235–239

BOETHIUS, 27–28

**BRIEF ANSWER, IN LEGAL
    MEMORANDUM,** 120–121, 132–134

BRIEFS, 5, 156
See also Appellate briefs

**(PRE-)BRIEFED CASES, FOR USE IN
    CLASS,** 58
See also Case briefs

BURKE, KENNETH, 119
A RHETORIC OF MOTIVES, 119

CALABRESI, GUIDO, 46

CAMPBELL, GEORGE, 35, 50, 157
PHILOSOPHY OF RHETORIC, 35

CAMPBELL, JOSEPH, 160–161
THE HERO WITH A THOUSAND FACES, 161

CANONS OF CONSTRUCTION
As part of statutory interpretation, 60

CANONS OF RHETORIC, 17, **47–49,** 255
Arrangement, 17, 30, 39, 47, 50
    In legal advocacy, 173
    In predictive writing, 119
Delivery, 17, 47–48, 255–266
Invention, 17, 30, 39, 47, 50, 69
Memory, 17, 47–48, 255–266
Style, 3, 17–18, 23, 27, 30–31, 35–36, 39,
    47–51, **221–254**

CAPITALIZE "COURT," WHEN TO, 238

CASE BRIEFS, FOR USE IN CLASS,
    11–12 and Appendix B

CASE LAW, 6, 42, 47, 53, 59–61, 82

CASE SYNTHESIS
See Rule synthesis

CASSIODORUS, 27

CATEGORICAL SYLLOGISM, 88, 92–93
See also Legal syllogism; Chapter 5,
    Appeals to Reason

CEREMONIAL SPEECH, 21, 47

CHAMALLAS, MARTHA, 44–45

CHASE, STUART, 222–223
THE POWER OF WORDS, 222

CHECKLIST FOR WRITING
Briefs, appellate, 216–219
Legal memoranda, 132–134
Style, 251–253

CHURCH, CHRISTIAN, 27, 29

CHURCH, ROMAN, 25

CICERO, 15, 22–25, 28, 30, 35, 38, 48,
    117, 120, 166, 221–222
DE INVENTIONE, 22

CLARITY OR CLEAR LEGAL
    WRITING, 222, 224–225, 235
Double negatives, avoid, 228
Elegant variation, avoid, 227,
Latin words and phrases, avoid, 225
Old-fashioned phrases, avoid, 226
Passive voice, use intentionally, 227
Redundant phrases, avoid, 226

CLEARLY ERRONEOUS, AS
    STANDARD OF REVIEW ON
    APPEAL, 203

CLIENT MEETINGS, 115, 256–260

COGNITIVE RHETORIC, 49, 52–53

COLLOQUIALISMS, AVOID, 238

COLONS, USE OF, 239, 241–242

COMBINE TOPIC SENTENCES WITH
    LAW, FOR CONCISENESS, 229

COMMAS AFTER INTRODUCTORY
    PHRASES, 241
Commas and semi-colons in a series, use of,
    242

COMMAS WITH COORDINATING
    CONJUNCTIONS, 241

COMMERCIAL OUTLINES, 58

COMMON LAW, 6, 45, 57, 60, 63, 80–83,
    104, 111

COMMON TOPICS, 70

COMMONLY CONFUSED WORDS, 246

COMPLAINTS, 156, 173–179
Format, 173
Sample complaint, 175

CONCISE OR CONCISENESS IN
    LEGAL WRITING, 3, 129, 132, 134,
    219, 228–229, 231–234, 240–241
Avoid long sentences, 229
Avoid nominalizations, 232

Combine topic sentences with conclusions
    or rules of law, 231
Devote no more space to an issue than it
    deserves, 230
Do not discuss non-relevant issues, 229
Do not explain what you intend to discuss
    or argue, 230
Do not summarize the history of the law,
    230
Omit unnecessary words and phrases, 232
Provide only relevant information in
    analogies, 233
State controlling rules of law just once, 230
Use explanatory parentheticals, 234

CONCURRING OPINION, 11

CONFLICT, AS PART OF CLIENT'S
    STORY, 110, 160–163, 174, 205

CONSTANTINE, EMPEROR, 25

CONSTITUTIONS, 53, 57, 61, 66, 72–73

CONSULT THE TOPICS, 72

CONTRACTIONS, AVOID, 136, 236, 246

CORAX, 18–19, 27
Elements of legal argument, 18

CORPORATIONS AND COURTS AS
    "ITS," 237

COUNTER-ARGUMENTS, 48, 116, 128,
    130–134, 139, 191, 210–212, 265
Anticipating, 131,
Denial of a factual allegation, 130
Disagreement with rule of law, 130
Minimizing impact, 132
Superseding argument, 131

COURTS
Federal, 62
State, 62

CREDIBILITY, 47, 53, 117–118, 166–168,
    170–171, 247

CRENSHAW, KIMBERLE, 44–45

CRITICAL LEGAL STUDIES, 42–43
Kennedy, Duncan, 43

CRITICAL RACE THEORY, 43–44
Bell, Derrick, 44
Lawrence, Charles, 44

DANGLING MODIFIERS, AVOID, 245

DASHES, EM, USE OF, 238

DATE FORM, PROPER, 239

DE INVENTIONE, 22–23, 28, 38, 69, 117,
    120, 166

DE NOVO, 150, 197, 203–204, 207

DE ORATORE, 22, 24, 28

DEDUCTION AND DEDUCTIVE
    REASONING, 21, 37, 41, 50, 79–80,
    87–89, 91, 93, 95, 97, 99, 103–104,
    109, 128
Fallacies in deductive reasoning, 97
    Begging the question, 101
    The book report (both premises
        missing), 97
    The deceptive hypothetical (denying
        the antecedent), 99
    Double negative proof (two no's don't
        make a yes), 100
    The fear of commitment (missing a
        conclusion), 98

DEEDS AND MORTGAGES, 5

DELAURENTIS, FRANCES, 169–170

DELIVERY, AS CANON OF
    RHETORIC, 17, 47–48, 255–266

DESCARTES, RENE, 31–35, 39
DISCOURSE ON METHOD AND THE
    MEDITATIONS, 32

DESCRIPTION, AS TYPE OF
    WRITING, 50

DIALECTIC, 20, 22, 29, 110

DIRECT QUOTES, USE OF, 236

DIRECTLY ADVERSE AUTHORITY,
    168

DISSENTING OPINION, 11

DISTRIBUTED TERM, 90, 94, 96

DRAFTING A PERSUASIVE
    STATEMENT OF THE CASE, 204

DUTY OF CANDOR TO THE
    TRIBUNAL, 166, 168

EARLY CHRISTIANITY, 24, 26

"EFFECT," USE OF, 246

ELBOW, PETER, 51
WRITING WITHOUT TEACHERS, 51

ELEGANT, STYLE, 223–224, 247, 249

ELEGANT VARIATION, 224, **227–228**

ELEMENTS
As organizing tool, 128, 136–137, 208
As parts of a memo, 48
Of a statute, 59, **82–87**
Of fiction, 110, 160
Of writing process, 49

ELOCUTIONARY MOVEMENT, 36

EM DASHES, 238

EMAIL, AS LEGAL ADVICE, 115, **135–
    141**
Format, 135
Sample email, 141

EMIG, JANET, 51

EMPIRICAL DATA, 114

EMPIRICISTS, 31
See also Bacon, Francis

EMPLOYMENT CONTRACTS, 5

EPISTEMOLOGY, 30–31, 34

ERASMUS, DESIDERIUS, 30

ETHOS
See Appeals to ethos

EXPLANATORY PARENTHETICALS,
    234–235

EXPOSITION, AS TYPE OF WRITING,
    50

EXPRESSIVISM, 49, 51, 53

FALLACIES IN DEDUCTIVE
    REASONING
See Deductive reasoning

FALSE DISPARAGEMENT STATUTE,
    IN TEXAS, 83

FAULTY GENERALIZATIONS
See Inductive reasoning

FEDERAL RULE OF APPELLATE
    PROCEDURE 28, 189, 191

FEDERALIST GOVERNMENT, 61

FEMINIST LEGAL THEORY, 44–45
Chamallas, Martha, 44
Frug, Mary Jo, 45
Halley, Janet, 45
MacKinnon, Catherine, 44
Matsuda, Mari, 45
Williams, Wendy, 44

FIGURES OF SPEECH, 27, 221, **247–251**
Alliteration, 247
Assonance, 247
Irony, 248
Metaphor, 248
Onomatopoeia, 250
Oxymoron, 250
Paradox, 250
Personification, 250
Simile, 250

FIRST, NOT FIRSTLY, 237

FIRST PERSON, AVOID, 235

FIVE-PARAGRAPH ESSAY, 50

FLOWER, LINDA, 51

FOLEY, BRIAN, 109

FORMS, MEDIEVAL, 28

FORMS OF PROOF
See Artistic and inartistic appeals

FRAMING THE LAW FROM YOUR
    CLIENT'S PERSPECTIVE, 157,
    163

FRAMING YOUR CLIENT'S STORY,
    157, 160–161, 204–205

FRANK, JEROME, 42

GARDNER, JAMES, A., 87–88, 95, 106

GILBERT, AUSTIN, 36, 58

GORGIAS
Plato's dialogue, title of, 21–22
Ten Great Attic Orators, one of the, 19, 25

GRAMMAR, PUNCTUATION, AND
    USAGE, 239–246
Avoid pronouns with ambiguous referents,
    243
Avoid splitting infinitives, 242
Colons and semi-colons outside quotation
    marks, 239
Commas after introductory phrases, 241
Commas and periods inside quotation
    marks, 239
Commas between independent clauses, 241
Commonly confused words, 246
Dangling modifiers, 245
Hyphens with compound adjectives, 242
Noun-verb and noun-pronoun agreement,
    244
Placement of "only," 245
Plural form for words ending in "s," 243
Possessive forms for words ending in "s,"
    243
Question and exclamation marks,
    placement in quotations, 240
Quotations of fifty or more words, 240
Semi-colons to join independent clauses,
    241
Semi-colons to separate items in a series,
    when to use, 242
"That" and "which," 242
Use of "hopefully" and "badly," 245

GREEN'S GROCER V. JANUS, 84–87,
    92–93, 97–101, 104, 106–109, 113,
    131, 164, 168–169

HALLEY, JANET, 45

HEADINGS
See Appellate briefs

HIERARCHY OF AUTHORITY, 61, 63

HIPPIAS, 19

HOBBES, THOMAS, 31

HOLMES, JUSTICE OLIVER
    WENDELL, 41

HOMER, 19

HOMILY, 25

"HOPEFULLY" AND "BADLY," 245

HORNBOOKS, 58

HOW ADVOCACY DIFFERS FROM
    ADVICE, 155

HUMANISTS, 18, 28, 30

HUME, DAVID, 31, 34, 116

HUTCHESON, JOSEPH, 105

HYPHENS WITH COMPOUND
    ADJECTIVES, 242

IDENTIFY THE ISSUE, 70–71, 128

"IMPLY," USE OF, 246

INARTISTIC APPEALS, 53

INDEPENDENT CLAUSES, 241

INDUCTION OR INDUCTIVE
    REASONING, 32, 34, 37, 50–51, 79–
    81, 83, 85, 87, 103–104, 109
Faulty generalizations, 86

INFORMAL LOGIC, 101

INSTITUTIO ORATORIO, 24, 28, 48,
    117, 166

INTRODUCTORY PHRASES, 241

INVENTION, 17, 28, 30, 39–40, 47, 50, 69,
    94, 222

IRONY, 117, 248, 253

ISOCRATES, 19, 25

"ITS," USE OF, 246

"IT'S," USE OF, 246

JENOFF, PAMELA, 54

JOSEPH, MIRIAM, SISTER, 39

JUDGMENT OF IMPORTANCE, 105–
    106, 108, 111–112

JUDICIAL DECISIONS, 6, 8, 10–12, 41–
    42, 45–46, 57, 62, 71, 80–82, 111
How to read, 11
Types, concurring, dissenting, majority,
    plurality, 11
Typical parts of, 10

JUDICIAL SPEECH, 15, 70

JUNG, CARL, 161

JURISDICTIONAL STATEMENT, 189–190, 193, 195, 216

KANT, IMMANUEL, 38

KENNEDY
Duncan, 43, 46
George, 25, 27–30, 34

KINNEAVY, JAMES, 15–16, 49
Language, 15, 49
Receiver, 16, 49
Speaker, 15, 49
A THEORY OF DISCOURSE, 16

KISSAM, PHILLIP, 52

KOZINSKI, JUDGE ALEX, 266

LANGDELL, CHRISTOPHER COLUMBUS, 37, 41

LARGE-SCALE ORGANIZATION
In briefs, 206
In legal memoranda, 127

LATIN FATHERS, 25

LATIN WORDS AND PHRASES, 223, 225

LAW AND ECONOMICS, 45–46
Calbresi, Guido, 46
Jolls, Christine, 46
Posner, Judge Richard A., 46
Sunstein, Cass R., 46
Thaler, Richard, 46

LAW BLOGS, 58

LAWRENCE, CHARLES, 43–44

LAWYER, THINKING LIKE A, 1

LEASES, 5, 223

LECTURES ON RHETORIC AND BELLE LETTRES, 36

LEGAL ADVICE, 3–4, 115–118
Bench memoranda, 146
Email, 135
Legal memoranda, 119
Opinion letters, 141

LEGAL ADVOCACY, 4, 155–172
Briefs, appellate, 188
Complaints, 173
Memorandum of points and authorities, 182
Motions, 179

LEGAL DICTIONARIES, 57

LEGAL ENCYCLOPEDIAS, 57, 66

LEGAL INSTRUMENTS, 3, 5

LEGAL ISSUES, 10, 23, 207

LEGAL MEMORANDA, 3–4, 16, 48, 100, **115–134,** 141, 148, 155, 164, 190–191, 209
Brief answer, 120
Checklist for writing, 132
Conclusion, 121
Discussion, 120
Heading, 119
Organization
    Large-scale, 127
    Small-scale, 128
Question presented, 119
Sample memo, 121 and Appendix C
Statement of facts, 120

LEGAL PERIODICALS, 57

LEGAL RESEARCH, 2–3, 5–7, 16, **65–70, 75,** 118, 260

LEGAL SYLLOGISM, 79–103, 231
Conclusion, 21, 79, 87–96
Distributed terms, 90, 94, 96
Major premise, 21, 87–96
Middle term, 89–96
Minor premise, 21, 87–96
Rules for validity, 89
Subject and predicate terms, 90

LEGAL TREATISES, 57

LEGAL WRITING CONVENTIONS, 134, 235–239
Avoid proper names when describing cited cases, 238
Capitalize "Court," when to, 238
Colloquialisms and slang, 238
Contractions, avoid, 236
Corporations and courts as "its," 237
Do not pose questions to the reader, 236
Em dashes, 238
First, not firstly, 237
First person, avoid, 235
Numerals, 238
The Oxford comma in a series, 237
Proper date form, 239
Spell judgment with one "e," 236
Supra, infra, and *see generally,* use of, 239
Use adverbs sparingly, 236
Use few direct quotes, 236
Use past tense to discuss cited cases, 237

LEIBNIZ, GOTTFRIED, 31

LETTER WRITING, 27–28

LEXISADVANCE, 202

LIMITED JURISDICTION, 61, 175

LINGUISTICS, 27

LLEWELLYN, KARL, 42
THE BRAMBLE BUSH, 42
Remarks on the Theory of Appellate Decision and the Rules or Canons

About How Statutes Are to Be Construed, 42

LOCKE, JOHN, 31, 50, 116, 157, 205
AN ESSAY CONCERNING HUMAN UNDERSTANDING, 116

LOGIC, 17–19, 21–23, 27, 29–32, 34–35, 39–41, 47, 50, 79–80, 87–89, 93, 95, 97, 101, 106, 109, 116, 155
Trivium, part of the, 17, 23, 27, 29, 36, 39

LOGOS, 39–40, 47, 79, 116, 255

LOW-COST ONLINE DATABASES, 68

LUNSFORD, ANDREA, 40

MAJOR PREMISE, 21, 87–96

MAJORITY OPINION, 11

MANDATORY AUTHORITY, 61, 119

MARGOLIS, ELLIE, 111–112

MATSUDA, MARI, 45

MEDIEVAL, 24, 27–29

MELLINKOFF, DAVID, 221–222

MEMORANDUM OF POINTS AND AUTHORITIES, 182–184
Format, 182
Sample memorandum of points and authorities, 183

MEMORY AND DELIVERY, 17, 48, **255–266**
Client meetings, 256
Oral advocacy, 260
Oral reporting, 255

METAPHOR, 15, 27, 109, **248–249**, 251

MIDDLE, STYLE OF WRITING, 48, 221, 224

MIDDLE AGES, 23, 27–29

MIDDLE TERM, OF SYLLOGISM, 89–96

MINI-ROADMAP, 213, 215–216

MINOR PREMISE, 21, 87–96

MIXED QUESTIONS OF FACT AND LAW, 23

MODEL RULES OF PROFESSIONAL CONDUCT, 118, 158, 164, 166, 168, 170–172, 258

MOTIONS, IN LEGAL ADVOCACY, 179–185
See also Arrangement

NARRATION, AS TYPE OF WRITING, 50

NARRATIVE REASONING, 109–111, 163, 251
Conflict, 110, 160–163, 174, 205
Elements of fiction, 110, 160
Framing your client's story, 157, 160–161, 204–205
Hero, 110, 160–163, 205
Plot, 110, 160, 162–163, 190, 205
Resolution, 110, 139, 160–162, 199, 205, 207

NATURE OF THE LEGAL ISSUES, 64

NEGATIVE, DOUBLE, 199

NEO-ARISTOTELIANISM, 50

NEO-CLASSICISTS, 35
Swift, Jonathan
THE BATTLE OF THE BOOKS, 35

NOMINALIZATIONS, 229, 232

NON-LEGAL SUPPORT OR POLICY ARGUMENTS
See Policy-based reasoning

NORMATIVE ARGUMENTS, 112

NOTICE PLEADING, 173

NOUN-VERB AND NOUN-PRONOUN AGREEMENT, 244

NUMBER, KEY, 68, 74, 204

NUMERALS, USE OF, 189, 212, 214, 238

OLBRECHTS-TYTECA, LUCIE, 40
THE NEW RHETORIC: A TREATISE ON ARGUMENTATION, 40

OLD-FASHIONED PHRASES, 224, 226

OMIT UNNECESSARY WORDS AND PHRASES, 229, 232

ONLINE DATABASES, 66–69
Free, 69
Low-cost, 68
Proprietary, 68

OPINION LETTERS, 3, 16, 115, 141, 143, 145
Format, 141
Sample opinion letter, 142

OPINIONS
See Judicial decisions

ORAL ADVOCACY, 260–261, 263, 265–266

ORAL ARGUMENT, 146–148, 154, 188, **260–265**
Etiquette, 264
How to prepare, 265
Typical format, 260

ORAL REPORTING, 255

ORATOR, CICERO, 22, 28, 48, 221–222

ORGANIZE AND ANALYZE AS YOU GO, 75, 77

ORGANON, NEW, 32

ORGANON, THE, 21, 27

OXYMORON, 250

PARADOX, 250

PARENTHETICALS, 134, 218–219, 234–235

PASSIVE VOICE, USE INTENTIONALLY, 224, 227–228

PAST TENSE TO DISCUSS CITED CASES, 237

PATHOS
See Appeals to pathos

PERELMAN, CHAIM, 39–40
THE NEW RHETORIC: A TREATISE ON ARGUMENTATION, 40
THE REALM OF RHETORIC, 40

PERSONIFICATION, 250

PERSUASIVE WRITING, 130, 132, 166, 236, 247, 251

PET BARN, INC. V. HOLMES, 85–87, 92, 111, 212, 233–235, 237–238

PHAEDRUS, 21

PLACEMENT OF COLONS AND SEMI-COLONS IN QUOTES, 239

PLACEMENT OF QUESTION AND EXCLAMATION MARKS IN QUOTES, 240

PLAIN ENGLISH FOR LAWYERS, 223, 232, 235

PLAIN ENGLISH MOVEMENT, 222, 224

PLATO, 2, **19–23**, 30, 33, 39–40, 52, 157

PLATO'S ACADEMY, 19

PLEADINGS, 4, 173–174, 195

PLOT, 110, 160, 162–163, 190, 205

PLURALITY OPINION, 11

POLICY-BASED REASONING, 5, 7, 12–13, 41, 46, 60, 81, 111–114, 124, 158, 163, 262

POLITICAL SPEECH, 15, 22

POPE, ALEXANDER, 35

POSITION PAPERS, 5

POSITIVISM, 50

POSSESSIVE, USE OF, 243, 246

POSTERIOR ANALYTICS, 21

PRACTICE-SPECIFIC NEWSLETTERS, 57

PRAGMATICS, 16

PREACHING, 25, 27

PREDICATE TERM, 90–91, 94, 96

PREDICTIVE WRITING, 115

PRIMARY SOURCES OF LAW, 57, 75, 239

PRIOR ANALYTICS, 21

PROFESSIONAL IDENTITY, 13, 170

PROFESSIONALISM, 118, 166, 168, 170–171

PRONOUNS WITH AMBIGUOUS REFERENTS, 243

PROPER NAMES, AVOID IN CASE DESCRIPTIONS, 238

PROPRIETARY ONLINE DATABASE, 68, 73, 75–76, 182, 202

PROTAGORAS, 19

PROVIDE ONLY RELEVANT INFORMATION IN ANALOGIES, 229, 252

PUBLIC POLICY, AS TOOL OF STATUTORY INTERPRETATION, 60

QUESTION OF FACT, 203–204

QUESTION OF LAW, 203

QUESTION PRESENTED, 119–121, 129, 132, 190

QUINTILIAN, 15, **24**, 28, 30, 35, 48, 79, 116–117, 157, 166
INSTITUTIO ORATORIO, 24

QUOTATION MARKS, 239–240

QUOTATIONS OF FIFTY WORDS OR MORE, 236, 240

RAMISM, 18, 30, 49

RAMUS, PETER, 30

RATIONALISM, 32, 34

RECURRING PROBLEMS IN ANALOGICAL REASONING, 106–109
The house of cards (relying on a case with an adverse outcome), 107
The missing link (too much missing information), 106
The problem with totality of the circumstances tests, 108

REALISM, 41–42
Frank, Jerome, 42
    LAW AND THE MODERN MIND, 42
Holmes, Justice Oliver Wendell, 41–42
Llewellyn, Karl, 42
    THE BRAMBLE BUSH, 42

REASONING, 79–113
Analogy, 103
The analytical paradigm, 79–80
Deduction, 87
Induction, 80
Narrative, 109
Policy-based, 111

REDUNDANT PHRASES, 224

REFER TO CORPORATIONS AND COURTS AS "ITS," 237

RENAISSANCE, 18, 27–30, 36, 222

REPORTERS, 7–8, 63, 66

RESEARCH PROCESS, THE, 69–77
Consult the topics, 72
Identify the issue, 70
Organize and analyze as you go, 75
Update the law, 75

RESOLUTION, AS PART OF CLIENT'S STORY, 110, 139, 160–162, 199, 205, 207

RESTATEMENTS, 57, 72

RHETORIC
Canons of, 17, **47–49,** 221, 255
Defined, 15–17
Distinguished from dialectic, 18, 19–20, 30, 35
As equivalent to philosophy, 39–40
As human interaction, 15
As part of the trivium, 17, 23, 27, 29, 39

RHETORICA AD CAIUS HERENNIUM, 22

ROADMAP, 120, 123, 127–128, 133, 135, 137, 144, 148, 185, 191, 197–198, 212–217, 230, 262

ROBBINS, RUTH ANNE, 109–110, 161–162

ROMAN EMPIRE, 24, 26–27, 75

RULE APPLICATION, 103

RULE SYNTHESIS, 79–83, 85, 103, 167, 219
Faulty generalizations, 86

RULES OF DISTRIBUTION, 89, 91

SAMPLE APPELLATE BRIEF, 192, 202, 248

SAMPLE BENCH MEMORANDUM, 148–149

SAMPLE COMPLAINT, 148, 175

SAMPLE EMAIL, 137

SAMPLE JUDICIAL DECISION, Appendix A

SAMPLE LEGAL MEMORANDUM, 121 and Appendix C

SAMPLE MEMORANDUM OF POINTS AND AUTHORITIES, 183

SCHOLASTICISM, 23, 29

SCIENTIFIC METHOD, 30, 37, 50, 80

SECOND SOPHISTS, 24–25, 29

SECONDARY AUTHORITY, 50, 57, 61, 66–68, 72–75, 160, 194, 239, 256

SECONDARY SOURCES OF LAW, 57–58, 68, 239

SEGAL, DAVID, 38

SEMANTICS, 16

SEMI-COLONS, USE OF, 239, 241–242, 252–253

SERMON, 25, 27
Thematic, 27

SHERIDAN, THOMAS, 36

SIMILE, 27, 221, 250–251

SMALL-SCALE ORGANIZATION
Briefs, 209
Memoranda, 128

SMITH, MICHAEL, 166

SOCIAL-EPISTEMIC RHETORIC, 52–53

SOCRATES, 19, 21, 88–91, 94

SOCRATIC TEACHING METHOD, 37

SOPHISTS, 2, 19–20, 24–25, 29

SOURCES OF LAW, 57, 61, 68, 73, 75–76, 81, 129, 239

SPECIAL TOPICS, 70

SPECIFIC TECHNIQUES FOR
    DRAFTING PERSUASIVE
    FACTS, 205

SPELL JUDGMENT WITH ONE "E,"
    236

SPINOZA, BARUCH, 31

STANDARD OF REVIEW, 147, 150, 191,
    193, 197, 202–204, 207, 217

STARBUCKS V. CSP, INC., CASES
Green's Grocer v. Janus, 84–87, 92–93, 97–
    101, 104, 106–109, 113, 131, 164,
    168–169
Pet Barn, Inc. v. Holmes, 85–87, 92, 111,
    212, 233–235, 237–238
Thomas Meats v. Safeway, 84, 87, 165, 167,
    235

STARE DECISIS, 63–64, 70, 74, 79, 103,
    105, 111, 169, 225, 249

STATE CONTROLLING RULES OF
    LAW JUST ONCE, 229

STATEMENT OF FACTS, 18, 120, 122,
    133, 150, 176, 190, 262

STATEMENT OF THE CASE, 147, 149,
    190, 193, 195, 204–205, 217, 261

STATEMENT OF THE ISSUES, 147–
    148, 217

STATUTES
Elements of, 59, 82–87
Format, typical, 58–59
        Damages, 59
        Definitions, 59
        Elements, 59, 82–87
        Exceptions, 59, 64, 73, 155
        Penalties, 59
        Purpose, 59
As inartistic appeals, 47, 53
As legal instruments, 5
As part of rule synthesis, 81–82
Tools for interpretation, 59–60
        Canons of construction, 60
        Case law, 59
        Context, 59
        Definitions, 59
        Legislative history, 60
        Plain meaning, 59–60, 85, 93, 125
        Public policy, 60

STUDY AIDS, 58

STYLE, IN LEGAL WRITING, 221–253
Checklist for style, 251
Elegant, 223–224
High, 48, 221–222
Low, 48, 221
Middle, 48, 221, 224

SUB-HEADINGS, 212

SUBJECT TERM, 89–91, 94, 96

SUBLIMITY, 31

SUMMARY OF ARGUMENT, 190, 193,
    196, 217–218

SUNSTEIN, CASS, R., 46, 105

SUPERSEDING ARGUMENT, 131

SUPRA, INFRA, AND *SEE
    GENERALLY*, 239

SWIFT, JONATHAN, 35

SYLLOGISM
See Legal syllogisms

SYNTHESIZED RULE, 80–86, 92–94, 97,
    110, 123–125, 128–129, 133–134,
    138–139, 164, 167, 210–211, 218, 231

TABLE OF AUTHORITIES, IN
    APPELLATE BRIEF, 189–190, 216

TABLE OF CONTENTS, IN
    APPELLATE BRIEF, 189, 212, 216

TASTE, 31, 35, 246

TESTIMONY, 42, 47, 70, 171, 188

"THAT" AND "WHICH," 242

THEAETETUS, 21

"THEIR," "THERE," AND "THEY'RE,"
    246

THEMATIC SERMON, 27

THEORIES OF WRITING, 50–52
Cognitive Rhetoric, 51
        Emig, Janet, 51
        Flower, Linda, 51
Current Traditionalism, 50
Expressivism, 51
        Elbow, Peter, 51
            WRITING WITHOUT TEACHERS,
                51
Neo-Aristotelianism, 50
Positivism, 50
Social-Epistemic Rhetoric, 52
        Berger, Linda, 52
        Berthoff, Ann, 52
        Bizzell, Patricia, 52
        Kissam, Philip, 52

THEORY OF THE CASE, 157–160, 174,
    206, 218, 249, 261

THINKING LIKE A LAWYER, 1

THOMAS MEATS V. SAFEWAY, 84, 87,
    165, 167

TOPIC SENTENCE, 50, 123, 125, 128–
    129, 132, 134, 186, 210–212, 218, 229,
    231, 251

TOULMIN, STEPHEN, 35, 101
USES OF ARGUMENT, 101
      Backing, 102
      Claim, 101
      Counterclaims, 101–102
      Data, 101
      Qualifier, 102
      Warrants, 102

TRIVIUM, THE, 17, 23, 27, 29, 36, 39, 224

TYPES OF RHETORIC, 21

TYPES OF WRITING: ARGUMENT, DESCRIPTION, EXPOSITION, NARRATION, 50

UNDISTRIBUTED TERM, 90

UPDATE THE LAW, 75, 204

USES OF ARGUMENT, 101

VALLA, LORENZO, 29

VELAS, RAMON, 115, 121–122, 142, 149, 158, 161–162, 174–175, 179, 181, 183, 192, 195, 201, 258, 261

VICKERS, BRIAN, 17

VICO, GIAMBATTISTA, 31, 34
NEW SCIENCE, 31

WALKER, JOHN, 36

WARD, JOHN, 35

WARRANT, 21, 101–103, 158, 163

WERESH, MELISSA, 168, 172

WESTLAW, 8, 67–68, 74, 76, 202, 204

WEST'S, 7, 10, 28

WHATELY, RICHARD, 35

WHITE PAPERS, 4–5

WILLIAMS, WENDY, 44

WILLS AND TRUSTS, 5

WILSON, THOMAS, 30
ART OF RHETORIC, 30

WITNESSES, 42, 260

WRITING WITHOUT TEACHERS, 51

WYDICK, RICHARD, 223